THE OPEN SIDE OF SECRECY

THE OPEN SIDE OF SECRECY

BRITAIN'S INTELLIGENCE AND
SECURITY COMMITTEE

ANTHONY GLEES
PHILIP H J DAVIES
AND
JOHN N L MORRISON

THE SOCIAL AFFAIRS UNIT

© The Social Affairs Unit 2006
All rights reserved

British Library Cataloguing in Publication Data
A catalogue record of this book is available from the British Library

All views expressed in this publication are those of the authors, not those
of the Social Affairs Unit, its Trustees, Advisers or Director

Printed and bound in the United Kingdom

ISBN 1-904863-16-7

Social Affairs Unit
314-322 Regent Street
London W1B 5SA
www.socialaffairsunit.org.uk

CONTENTS

GLOSSARY		7
FOREWORD		11
CHAPTER 1	INTRODUCTION	13
CHAPTER 2	DEVELOPMENT AND WORK OF THE COMMITTEE	31
CHAPTER 3	IS INTELLIGENCE OVERSIGHT REALLY NECESSARY?	51
CHAPTER 4	THE ISC IN ACTION – 10 YEARS OF OVERSIGHT UK-STYLE	91
CHAPTER 5	THE ISC AND THE ALTERNATIVE RATIONALE FOR OVERSIGHT	163
CHAPTER 6	IMPROVING THE ISC – THE NEXT DECADE	173

GLOSSARY OF ACRONYMS AND ABBREVIATIONS

BBC	British Broadcasting Company (UK)
CIA	Central Intelligence Agency (US)
CBW	Chemical and Biological Weapons
CDI	Chief of Defence Intelligence (UK)
COBRA	Cabinet Office Briefing Room 'A' (UK)
CSI	Ministerial Committee on the Intelligence Services (UK)
CSIS	Canadian Security Intelligence Service (Canada)
DCI	Director of Central Intelligence (US)
DIS	Defence Intelligence Staff (UK)
DISC	Defence Intelligence and Security Centre (part of DIS)
DoD	Department of Defense (US)
DNI	Director of National Intelligence (US)
FAC	Foreign Affairs Committee (UK)
FBI	Federal Bureau of Investigation (US)
FCO	Foreign and Commonwealth Office (UK)
FOA	Foreign Office Advisor (to SIS)
GCHQ	Government Communications Headquarters (UK)
GPO	General Post Office (UK)
GRU	*Glavnoe Razvedyvatel'noe Upravlenie* ('Main Intelligence Directorate' – military intelligence in USSR and (subsequently) Russia)
HAC	Home Affairs Committee (UK)
HCDC	House of Commons Defence Committee (UK)
HMG	Her Majesty's Government (UK)
HMSO	Her Majesty's Stationery Office (UK)
HPSCI	House Permanent Select Committee on Intelligence (US)

IOCA	Interception of Communications Act 1985
IAEA	International Atomic Energy Authority
IGIS	Inspector-General of Intelligence and Security (Australia)
ISA	Intelligence Services Act 1994
ISC	Intelligence and Security Committee (UK)
IT	Information Technology
JARIC	Joint Air Reconnaissance Intelligence Centre (part of DIS)
JIC	Joint Intelligence Committee (UK)
JTAC	Joint Intelligence Analysis Centre (UK)
KGB	*Komitet Gosudarstvennoy Bezopasnosti* ('State Security Committee' – espionage and counter-espionage agency of the former USSR)
MoD	Ministry of Defence (UK)
NAO	National Audit Office (UK)
NATO	North Atlantic Treaty Organization
NCIS	National Criminal Intelligence Service (UK)
NIRP	National Intelligence Requirements Process
NCS	National Crime Squad (UK)
NSA	National Security Agency (US)
OSA	Official Secrets Act 1989
PC	Privy Counsellor (UK)
PJHQ	Permanent Joint Headquarters (UK)
PM	Prime Minister
PSIS	Permanent Secretaries' Committee on the Intelligence Services (UK)
PUS	Permanent Under Secretary
R&D	Research and Development
RCMP	Royal Canadian Mounted Police (Canada)
RCMP/SS	Royal Canadian Mounted Police Security Service (Canada)
RIPA	Regulation of Investigatory Powers Act 2000
RSPCA	Royal Society for the Prevention of Cruelty to Animals (UK)
RUSI	Royal United Services Institute (UK)
SIA	Single Intelligence Account (UK)
SIS	Secret Intelligence Service (UK)

SIV	Single Intelligence Vote (UK)
SO	Official Committee on Security (UK)
SOCA	Serious Organised Crime Agency (UK)
SSA	Security Service Act 1989
SSCI	Senate Select Committee on Intelligence (US)
UNSCOM	United Nations Special Committee (for CBW-related inspections in Iraq)
WMD	Weapons of Mass Destruction

FOREWORD

The Intelligence and Security Committee (ISC) is now over 11 years old. Its statutory task is to oversee the UK's three intelligence and security Agencies – the Secret Intelligence Service (SIS or 'MI6'), the Security Service ('MI5') and the Government Communications Headquarters (GCHQ). How well has it carried out its work, and has it identified the causes of 'intelligence failures' to ensure they are not repeated? Has it contributed to the security of the UK and its citizens? As the Chancellor of the Exchequer, the Rt Hon Gordon Brown MP, put it in his keynote speech of 13 February 2006, referring to the London terrorist attacks of 2005:

> As July 7th solemnly and starkly reminds us, the first responsibility of a government is to protect its citizens, keep people safe and ensure their security.

In the same speech he hinted cryptically that there might be significant changes to the UK intelligence community and its oversight mechanisms:

> …we will examine the case for a single security budget, assessing also how in this new world we secure the best coordination in delivery and accountability – including the appointment of the relevant committees and their investigative power: at all points building trust in a tough security regime through necessary accountability.

This therefore seems an appropriate moment to review the performance of the ISC and consider how it might be improved. Since its creation in 1994 the Committee has evolved, extending its effective authority to cover the whole of the core UK intelligence community and producing reports on critical intelligence issues. It is therefore surprising how little academic attention the ISC has received; to the best of our knowledge this is the first ever in-depth examination of the Committee and how it exercises its intelligence oversight responsibilities. We have tried throughout to be critically constructive.

Our studies have made us very conscious of how much more could have been mined from the first three Committees' nineteen reports (eleven annual, eight special); at the time of writing, the current ISC – the fourth – has yet to issue its first report. We have also focused rather tightly on the ISC itself; there is more work to be done in considering its development alongside that of the three UK intelligence and security Agencies, as well as other elements of the UK intelligence machine, such as the Joint Intelligence Committee (JIC) and the Defence Intelligence Staff (DIS).

We are indebted to the chair of the first two Committees (1994–97 and 1997–2001), the Rt Hon The Lord King of Bridgwater CH PC; the chair of the third committee (2001–05), the Rt Hon Baroness Taylor of Bolton PC, and Sir David Omand GCB, the first Security and Intelligence Co-ordinator in the Cabinet Office from 2002–05, all of whom were good enough to provide us with on-the-record interviews that provided a unique insight into the ISC's work and its relationships with the Agencies and government. We trust they will forgive us for stripping all three of them (as well as others) of their full titles and honours in the main text, in the interests of clarity and brevity. We are also grateful to other former senior 'insiders' who spoke to us on condition of confidentiality.

Finally, it should be noted that one of the authors, John Morrison, had dealings with the ISC both as a civil servant prior to his retirement in 1999 and, under contract as a consultant, from 1999 to 2004 as the Committee's Investigator. He would like to make it clear that this book contains no confidential information he obtained in either role; his contribution has relied entirely on open (and cited) sources. Nor did he draft those sections of the book dealing with his controversial departure from the Committee's employ.

CHAPTER 1

INTRODUCTION

A man's most open actions have a secret side to them.
Joseph Conrad, *Under Western Eyes*

**INTELLIGENCE OVERSIGHT:
CURRENT AND FUTURE CHALLENGES**

The above statement by Conrad's character Razumov can just as well be applied to governments: they strive to obtain the secrets of others while protecting their own. Secrecy cuts both ways: what you do *not* know can hurt you, and therefore a government's policies and actions must be based upon as complete an information set as possible. But, equally, preserving your secrets gives you an edge over your foreign enemies and rivals. Thus the need for intelligence and security agencies – is there a country in the world without them? – the 'secret side' of government.

But the very secrecy these agencies require to carry out their offensive and defensive tasks can create concerns about their activities. Are they, at worst, abusing their positions? If not, are they doing their work effectively and providing value for money? Could they be improved and, if so, how? In many countries the parliament and public receive no answer to such questions, but in the UK and other liberal democracies mechanisms have been set up outside the government machine to ensure accountability – what we have dubbed 'the open side of secrecy'. In this book we look at the most important 'oversight' body in the UK, the Intelligence and Security Committee (ISC), its performance over its first 10-plus years, and the challenges facing it in the next decade.[1]

The May 2005 UK general election resulted in a New Labour government facing a daunting array of long-term constitutional and political problems. But the murderous attacks on London of 7 July and 21 July 2005 (7/7 and 21/7 in popular parlance) mean that, in the short to medium term, attention is likely to be focused on another area of policy altogether – the delivery of security through measures to guard Britain against future terrorist attacks. As the

Chancellor of the Exchequer, the Rt Hon Gordon Brown, said in his heavily trailed keynote policy speech of 13 February 2006:

> Addressing the reality, causes and roots of international terrorism is one of the greatest new challenges of our times. Of course all the great challenges of globalisation are important, but upon meeting and overcoming the challenge of global terrorism all else we value depends.[2]

Attention has once more been focused on the activities, policies and effectiveness of the UK's three core intelligence and security organizations: the Secret Intelligence Service (SIS, commonly known as 'MI6'), the Security Service ('MI5') and the Government Communications Headquarters (GCHQ). The country has been told over and over again that the fight against terrorism must be 'intelligence led'; these Agencies[3] and their staffs, together with the Special Branches of Britain's police forces, are the front-line troops in this fight.

Meanwhile, in the background, like a toothache that will not go away, the aftermath of the second Gulf war continues as an irritant for the government. The public justification for the invasion of Iraq was that Saddam possessed weapons of mass destruction (WMD), and the public was told that this had been irrefutably proved by intelligence. We now know that Saddam had *no* WMD, and that the underlying intelligence was fatally flawed. The failings of UK intelligence were elegantly dissected in the Butler Report,[4] whose findings extended to the Defence Intelligence Staff (DIS) and the Joint Intelligence Committee (JIC), bringing into question the competence of the whole UK intelligence community. For the first time in history, Britain had used intelligence assessments as the public justification for invading a sovereign state – and those assessments were wrong. The public could be excused for questioning the abilities of the Agencies and the UK intelligence community as a whole: if they could get it so wrong over Iraq, why should they be trusted over issues nearer home, above all the fight against terrorism?

This point was made explicitly by Lord Carlile of Berriew, since 2001 the government's independent reviewer of terrorism legislation, who said (in February 2006 evidence to the House of Commons Home Affairs Committee) that the lack of public trust in the security and intelligence services over the terrorist threat stemmed directly from the way the government made the case for war in Iraq:

The trust issue has been very damaged by the intelligence information connected with the Iraq war which is perceived, rightly or wrongly, to be inaccurate.[5]

Any state that, like Britain, considers itself a mature liberal democracy must provide some formal means of auditing the work of its intelligence and security agencies, keeping an official eye on their performance, and accounting for it to the public in some format or other. This, in essence, is what 'oversight' is about. At least nineteen states have some form of intelligence oversight,[6] though in many it is of limited effectiveness and vulnerable to government pressure. Here, such a task is not merely a government responsibility but is subject to review by the ISC – a committee of parliamentarians usually (but, as we shall see, inaccurately) referred to as the 'parliamentary' Intelligence and Security Committee.

THE COMMITTEE'S TASKS FOR THE NEXT DECADE

The ISC is now in its fourth incarnation under its third chair, Paul Murphy.[7] It is the right time not just to reflect on its first decade of work, but to look forward to its next ten years, to consider its successes and failures and areas of future activity, identifiable both by obvious national need and by its statutory responsibilities, as well as the manner in which it conducts its business. Among the most pressing issues the new ISC will need to address will be the failure to foresee the attacks of 7/7 and 21/7 and the aftermath of the flawed intelligence and assessments on Iraqi WMD. This latter issue is by no means dead: the outgoing Committee pledged to monitor the reforms recommended in the Butler Report (and accepted by the government), and it would be strange if the new Committee did not honour that pledge.

On the terrorism issue, the Committee is examining the circumstances surrounding the terrorist attacks of July 2005. While it has not revealed the detailed thrust of its inquiry, it may be expected to pay particular attention to two main questions. First, why was there no intelligence whatsoever providing warning of these attacks, as has been admitted by both the home secretary and Commissioner of the Metropolitan Police Sir Ian Blair? Only the month before, Sir Ian had approvingly quoted a description of the Metropolitan Police by Her Majesty's Inspectorate of Constabulary as '"The envy of the world" when it comes to counter-terrorism', and had cited the International Olympic Committee's view of his force as 'the gold standard for world policing'.[8] Does this suggest a dangerous smugness prior to the 7/7 attacks?

Second, why was it that, several days prior to 7/7, the Joint Terrorism Analysis Centre (JTAC, based in the Security Service headquarters, Thames House) downgraded the threat level from 'severe general' to 'substantial', the fourth point on a five-point threat-calibration scale?[9] The top priority for the ISC will always be to ask 'what went wrong?', and the 7/7 and 21/7 attacks are plainly the most important single item on the new ISC's agenda. But here, it must be said, there is a disquieting parallel to the experience of the third Committee, appointed in 2001, which was immediately thrown into investigating the aftermath of the '9/11' terrorist attacks on New York and Washington before it had a chance to settle into its wider role.

It should be stressed that the Iraqi WMD problems with which the ISC must wrestle do not, in themselves, stem from the policy decision to go to war with Iraq. Rather, as has already been noted, they result from the repeated government statements prior to the invasion that the policy decision to go to war was the inevitable outcome of intelligence reports and assessments that concluded that Iraq possessed WMD. The government went to the unprecedented lengths of producing an extensive unclassified dossier based on JIC assessments.[10] In his introduction to the dossier, Prime Minister Tony Blair stated forcefully:

> What I believe *the assessed intelligence has established beyond doubt* is that Saddam has continued to produce chemical and biological weapons, that he continues in his efforts to develop nuclear weapons, and that he has been able to extend the range of his ballistic missile programme. I also believe that, as stated in the document, Saddam will now do his utmost to try to conceal his weapons from UN inspectors.
>
> *The picture presented to me by the JIC in recent months has become more not less worrying.* It is clear that, despite sanctions, the policy of containment has not worked sufficiently well to prevent Saddam from developing these weapons.
>
> *I am in no doubt that the threat is serious and current*, that he has made progress on WMD, and that he has to be stopped. [our emphases]

Yet, as was discovered after the war, for the best part of a decade Saddam Hussein had possessed *no* WMD capability whatsoever – the raw and assessed intelligence was wrong; the JIC assessments, while incorrect, had *not* presented an increasingly worrying picture, and there was *no* 'serious and current' threat from Saddam's (non-existent) WMD.

That is about as bad as it gets in the world of intelligence. Certainly, it had been a serious mistake to fail to predict the Ardennes offensive in late 1944, or the invasion of the Falklands in 1982. But these errors consisted of British intelligence missing things that could have been spotted had it looked hard enough. The failure in the case of Iraq was to look very hard – and then discover things that were not there. It will take many years, and arguably a fundamental and radical reform of British intelligence (so far not even hinted at), before public faith in the competence of the Agencies and the assessment processes is fully restored.

Yet a blanket indictment of the whole of the UK intelligence community would be foolish. In the case of Iraqi WMD, the most serious criticisms can, at present, be justly directed at only one part of it – SIS. It is true that the other two agencies, the Security Service and GCHQ, were equal partners, together with their fellow JIC members, in the flawed judgements on Iraqi WMD. The JIC is, after all, the top-level forum, which should ensure that the UK intelligence community as a whole reaches a consensus view that gets as close as possible to the truth. As for terrorism, the Security Service seems to have dropped its guard: its obvious lack of intelligence about 7/7 and 21/7, added to JTAC's inability to correctly calibrate the threat level, fully justifies the Committee's inquiry.

All three Agencies have been criticized by the ISC over the years on various grounds; some of these failings are explored in Chapter 4. Public confidence in the Agencies has also been undermined to some extent by 'whistle-blowing' revelations from current and former staff. Richard Tomlinson (SIS), David Shayler (Security Service) and Katharine Gun (GCHQ) have portrayed themselves as principled opponents of the malpractices of the Agencies, and the press have generally shown themselves ready to publicize their views, sometimes (though by no means always) with sympathy.

The government therefore needs both to repair any failings in the UK intelligence system and to restore public faith in the institutions of British intelligence, which, after all, cost the taxpayer something in excess of £1.5 billion each year.[11] But how will the public know whether whatever repairs it undertakes have been good enough? By their nature, the UK intelligence and security Agencies must operate in secrecy – the normal ways of judging political success or failure do not apply. While it could be said that public trust in the intelligence services can be built up by evidence of their successes, even here there are problems. Successes do exist: former Commissioner of the Metropolitan Police Lord Stevens has stated that at least six terror attacks prior to 7/7 were thwarted, while Gordon Brown subsequently revealed that three attack plans threatening Britain had been foiled since 21/7.[12] As Percy Cradock pointed out some years ago, there are often things about which the public can know nothing, because they are catastrophes that do not take place.[13] Yet, as Sir Michael Quinlan has observed, 'The most measurable things about intelligence are usually to be found in its failures.'[14]

THE INTRICACIES AND PARADOXES OF OVERSIGHT

The government's substantive and presentational tasks are complicated by the ever-present insistence on 'transparency and openness' in governance; we live in an audit culture. Indeed, audit has now become a formal requirement throughout the government machine – and one from which the three Agencies are not excused – to be executed both within departments and by the wholly independent National Audit Office.[15] However, unlike almost every other area of government, the intelligence and security services would appear to face an impossible job in providing convincing audit to the public at large. This is because transparency is not just about *process*, but is also, and far more, about *content*. Content in the context of the secret Agencies is, however, about *secrecy* not *transparency*. Nor can it be otherwise, and in this sense genuine public transparency in political terms can never be achieved. So how can the public be convinced that there is an effective audit – 'oversight' – of things they can never see or judge?

The British solution to this unique political conundrum was to set up a unique committee – the Intelligence and Security Committee (ISC) – under the statutory authority of the Intelligence Services Act 1994 (ISA 1994). In the following chapter we review the ISC's origins in the early 1990s and its subsequent development, outline its support structure, and describe its *modus operandi* and outputs over the past decade and more. Before proceeding to consider its effectiveness, however, we felt it necessary to address the key issues involved in the oversight of intelligence, and Chapter 3 therefore tackles the fundamental question: 'Is oversight of intelligence really necessary?' We then move on to review the ISC's work over the past decade in more detail, assess the possible justifications for its existence and activities, and finally consider ways in which the Committee might direct its efforts and become more effective in future.

In considering the ISC's track record, it should be recalled that it is not the only parliamentary committee with legitimate concerns in intelligence matters. The Foreign, Home and Defence select committees all have considerable interest in them as well – and all of them have engaged in turf battles with the ISC. The ISC, however, has unique duties and a unique location in British governance. As commentators often fail to note, the ISC is a quite special committee of parliamentarians. (It is definitely *not* a select committee, though many refer to it as such.) And, unlike any other parliamentary committee, the ISC operates within what is known as the 'ring of secrecy'.[16] Its members '...are appointed by, and report directly to, the Prime Minister and through him to Parliament by the publication of the Committee's Report' and are 'notified'[17] under the 1989 Official Secrets Act.[18] Although the names of possible candidates will, presumably, be submitted for scrutiny to the whips' offices, and although (like ministers) members do not undergo formal Developed Vetting,[19] it may be assumed that there are informal checks with the Security Service to ensure that nominees are suitable to serve on the Committee.

The process by which the ISC reports to Parliament and the British people is also highly unusual. As we have noted, it does not actually report direct to Parliament but to the prime minister of the day. Having told the prime minister what it has found, in the wording traditionally used by the Committee in the introduction to its annual reports (it varies somewhat from report to report), the ISC agrees to the exclusion of sensitive material before the report's publication as a Command Paper:

> When laying a Report before Parliament, the Prime Minister, in consultation with the Committee, excludes any part of the Report (indicated by the *** in the text) that would be prejudicial to the continuing discharge of the functions of the three intelligence and security Agencies. To date, no material has been excluded without the Committee's consent.[20]

The above is from the Committee's 2004–05 annual report; in practice, it may be assumed that, in this context, the words 'the Prime Minister' are shorthand for 'UK officialdom', and, in particular, the three Agencies who provide the main focus for the Committee's work. It indicates that, since its formation, the ISC has never objected to a prime minister's request for exclusions from the report – we will consider the implications of this later. It must also be asked whether copious deletions of text prove the ISC is fulfilling its public role by reviewing sensitive subjects in depth, or whether they allow the Agencies to conceal matters that should be public knowledge. (The first ISC chairman, Tom King, was in no doubt that the former was the case: when challenged by reporters about the increasing number of asterisks in the Committee's annual reports – particularly on the Agencies' finances – he maintained that they simply served to show how much more detail the ISC was now getting into.) Whatever the case, it may be questioned whether the asterisks provide a reliable guide to the volume of material redacted – how much is contained in a sentence or paragraph represented only by ***?

Many of the redactions in the published annual reports involve the deletion of budgetary information: there are whole pages of tables composed entirely of asterisks. In terms of the Agencies' budgets, while Parliament and public see only the total allocation for all three Agencies – the Single Intelligence Account – in Tom King's words:

> Although only asterisks are shown in the ISC reports, the actual figures had been seen by the ISC, down to such details as the total payments to agents.[21]

'Secrecy' and 'transparency' are concepts fundamentally opposed to each other. We will consider later whether the ISC can really be shown to have overcome the deep paradoxes implicit in seeking publicly accountable access to the closed world of secrets. The Committee regularly emphasizes (as it has done in various forms since its formation) the extent of its insight into this hermetic world:

> The members are notified under the Official Secrets Act 1989 and, as such, operate within 'the ring of secrecy'. The Committee sees significant amounts of classified material in carrying out its duties and it takes evidence from Cabinet Ministers and senior officials – all of which is used to formulate its reports.[22]

It is much to the ISC's credit that, although its members know a very great deal about Britain's secrets, to date none has ever leaked them.

KEY ISSUES REGARDING THE ISC

Some eleven years after the inception of the ISC, two central issues must now be asked about it – and, via the ISC, about the way in which Britain uses intelligence to lead its most important national policies. But before addressing them, we must repeat the quote in our foreword from Gordon Brown's 13 February 2006 speech to the Royal United Services Institute (RUSI):

> …we will examine the case for a single security budget, assessing also how in this new world we secure the best coordination in delivery and accountability – including the appointment of the relevant committees and their investigative power: at all points building trust in a tough security regime through necessary accountability.

This is nothing if not gnomic: given the number of organizations with a finger in the security pie, how could parts of their budgets be extracted and amalgamated to form 'a single security budget'? Is the intention simply to show how much is being spent on security across the board – an indicative rather than a real budget – and, if so, what purpose would this serve? Or was the chancellor hinting at the formation of a 'Ministry of Intelligence and Security' – a concept that has often been mooted (and invariably rejected) over the years?

And what did he mean by 'examine…the appointment of the relevant committees and their investigative power'? Was this meant to include the ISC, even though any change in its procedures and powers would require new legislation? Or was this just a 'tick in the box' insertion for the purposes of the speech? We simply do not know the answers to such questions, and we have therefore assumed that the ISC will continue with its current responsibilities for the foreseeable future – however short that may turn out to be.

Before looking at the key issues facing the ISC now and in the future, it is worth briefly reviewing its development. In its initial phase, from 1994–97, the Committee had to establish itself and its authority. This was hardly surprising. Throughout the world, and especially in mature democracies, intelligence oversight has taken many forms and has many varied duties. We do not examine them here because it is plain that British oversight is derived chiefly from the North American experience. What is more, the British experience of parliamentary democracy was far happier than that of many other countries, and the faith placed in government institutions was correspondingly higher. Nevertheless, the UK Agencies and the intelligence community as a whole had no experience of oversight (nor, self-evidently, had the ISC as a collective entity, though some members had been ministers responsible for authorizing and overseeing intelligence work). The initial phase was, therefore, one of exploration and accommodation on both sides.

In its second incarnation, from 1997–2001, the ISC began to flex its muscles under the continued robust leadership of Tom King, extending its *de facto* authority and, in the Mitrokhin inquiry, obtaining unique investigative powers. The Committee's third phase, from 2001–05, began immediately after the terrorist attacks of 11 September 2001, and the new Committee, much more than its predecessors, appeared driven by external events rather than by any agenda of its own. It also began to move into the world of substantive intelligence: the ISC's second chair, Ann Taylor, said in her 2002–03 report:

> The Committee is grateful to the JIC Chairman and to 'C' [the chief of the Secret Intelligence Service, then Sir Richard Dearlove] for the regular briefings by which we have been kept up to date before, and during, the military action against Iraq, as it was intelligence that indicated the Iraqis were continuing to produce WMD and their delivery means.[23]

This series of briefings by the JIC chairman and 'C' inevitably raises questions about the role of the Committee, both objectively and as seen by its members. Was the ISC competent to evaluate the single-source and assessed intelligence they were being fed? If not, what purpose did the briefings serve? If the ISC felt they ought to receive briefings on substantive intelligence and assessments (not a responsibility assigned to them in ISA 1994) should their approach not have been more methodical and critical? A cardinal tenet of intelligence (though usually applied in a security context) is that intelligence should be provided on a 'need to know', not a 'nice to know' basis. In this instance, it could be argued that the Committee was operating in the latter mode.

Returning to our two key issues, the first has to do with the ISC's performance over the past ten years. Has the ISC actually 'delivered'? Why did ten years of parliamentary 'oversight' not alert the public to the shortcomings within British intelligence that led directly to the Iraqi WMD debacle? What, a cynic might ask, is the point of the ISC if it could not prevent this?

The second issue facing the ISC at this critical time for British intelligence and security is, of course, the future. Will the ISC deliver more successfully in the years to come? On the micro level, how can the British public, through the ISC, be assured that the changes, some of which are already being implemented today as a result of the Butler Report, will improve matters? On the macro level, how can the ISC help improve the quality of British secret intelligence gathering, help sustain our security and restore public trust both in the intelligence services and in the government's management of them?

THE QUESTION OF TRUST

It is not just our intelligence Agencies or our governments that we need to trust. We also need to trust the ISC to oversee them properly, on our behalf. This is a vital national requirement, partly because of the central role the Agencies play in our national and international political life, and partly (and as a consequence of this) because they possess real power in today's political environment. Major yet secret institutions of state have grown out of the small offices and adjunct departments of the last hundred years or so. While the reputation of individual agencies has waxed and waned – SIS was badly damaged by Iraq, whereas, until the attacks of July 2005, the Security Service was riding the crest of a wave – our secret institutions will always be a significant *sub rosa* force in our national life. If the Agencies are to function properly in a democracy, they must be trusted.

As the first ISC chair, Tom King, put it in the final words of his trenchant foreword to the ISC's 1997–98 report:

> The Agencies face [their] tasks in a new environment of greater openness and accountability...Overall it is vital that public confidence is maintained in the Agencies. At times of grave national threat, their value is readily accepted. At other times, in the face of a bungled operation or security lapse, public confidence can be very fragile. That is the inevitable consequence of operating within the 'ring of secrecy' which prevents a more balanced public view of their activities and their value. The public must be confident that there is adequate

> independent scrutiny and democratic accountability on their
> behalf, by people within that 'ring of secrecy'.
>   That is the task of this Committee.[24]

It is, of course, interesting that Tom King accepts that the 'ring of secrecy' militates *against* what he calls a 'balanced' public view, a point to which we return below. King had earlier emphasized the difficult nature of the ISC's duties:

> By their nature, they [the Agencies] have not been exposed
> to detailed public examination, or close scrutiny by the media.
> Indeed, until only recently the very existence of the Secret
> Intelligence Service (SIS) and the Security Service was not
> admitted...After nearly 90 years in operation, it is only in
> the last four that the Government has admitted to the
> existence of SIS ... The public declaration of the existence
> of the Agencies brought with it issues of democratic
> accountability for their activities.[25]

Trust in the *activities* of the Agencies is one thing. Public trust in the government's *management* of them is another, entirely different question. Yet here, too, the ISC has a vital job to do. We may believe that any administration should develop strong and internally consistent governmental systems, processes and procedures if it is to use intelligence successfully. But the only way we in the UK can actually know whether this has been done is through the ISC. In Chapter 4 we consider how the ISC has developed over the years and how it has handled a number of key issues. During its life the Committee has trained its spotlight on a wide range of subjects, not all addressed here, though the focus has sometimes appeared to depend more on the concerns of individual members at the time than on a coherent programme of long-term work.

We will argue that the ISC has done some things that worked well, and other things that did not work so well – or indeed at all; that it has addressed many real intelligence and security concerns but has ignored, or been diverted away from, certain others. Some of its shortcomings may be attributable, we suggest, to the governmental structure in which the ISC is obliged to operate, its complex presence inside the ring of secrecy and a tendency for the current prime minister (Tony Blair) to believe that the ultimate authority of No. 10 Downing Street (which is a constitutional and political fact of life) must be reflected, to a possibly inappropriate degree, at the intelligence-gathering and analysis end of the policy-making process.

Some of this may have to do with the fact that the prime minister himself appoints the chair of the ISC and (albeit in consultation with the opposition parties) its members; furthermore, because the ISC is a high-profile committee, appointment to it could easily be perceived as a political consolation prize for those who have lost high office or are being told they will never gain it.

AUDITING THE MANAGEMENT OF THE AGENCIES

The ISC's terms of reference, as laid down in ISA 1994, require it to examine the 'expenditure, administration and policy' of SIS, the Security Service and GCHQ, as described in the following chapter. For nearly a decade, it appeared to be on top of this task, congratulating the Agencies on their successes and criticizing their shortcomings in measured terms. Then came the fiasco of Iraqi WMD, where the supposedly sound intelligence justifying – indeed supposedly requiring – the invasion of Iraq was shown to be largely wrong. Clearly there had been major problems with both the raw intelligence – in this case human intelligence or 'Humint' – and the assessment process. Why had the ISC not spotted these problems?

As one former senior intelligence officer has pointed out, assessing the weapons capability of a hostile or potentially hostile power is bog-standard intelligence work.[26] No one was asking the JIC to predict Saddam's future intentions or future stockpiles, but rather to assess his current weapons stockpiles and programmes – something that, during the Cold War years (but also previously), the JIC appeared to have done well. The fact that no British intelligence chiefs lost their posts did not mean that drastic measures were not deemed necessary; Lord Butler's report implied that, without such measures, the public would have little reason to have confidence in the government's ability to manage intelligence issues with any degree of success. Indeed, as we shall see, the ISC itself persistently suggested that the government had not been observing due process in this area, as shown by its continuing failure to convene meetings of the Ministerial Committee on the Intelligence Services (CSI).

Thanks to the Butler Report, some changes are already being enacted in the governance of the British intelligence and security community. Changes are also being made to the systems and mechanisms by which secret intelligence is fed into the policy-making arena occupied by Cabinet ministers, with the prime minister at their head. But those that have been started are not complete, and, as we suggest in this book, more must follow.

That is yet another task for the ISC. A good and well-defined line of management in intelligence and security affairs is not, of course, an automatic guarantee of intelligence successes, but it can help guard against intelligence failures. The ISC as an entity is well placed to judge these matters, since so much of its work over the past ten years has been devoted to the study of intelligence and security systems, processes and procedures. Yet, as we shall see, it is worrying that there is still evidence of fundamental problems in Whitehall's management of intelligence. There must also be doubts about the ability of the fourth Committee, appointed in July 2005, to grapple with these problems. Not only are six of its nine members first-timers, but it will inevitably have been preoccupied with its inquiry into the July 2005 London terrorist attacks, as its predecessor was by the impact of 9/11 shortly after that Committee's formation.

As we have noted, Gordon Brown's speech leaves a slight question mark hanging over the Committee. Yet, even if it were to be abolished, the ISC's functions would still have to be exercised in some fashion because the public (and its elected representatives in Parliament) will henceforth continue to demand transparency. Since they cannot actually be granted it in the measure that they might wish, a mediator between themselves and the secret Agencies will always be required. Even if the public accepts the need for secrecy in the work of the Agencies, it would be absurd to imagine, in the aftermath of the Iraq war, that any British government would find it possible to curtail, let alone abolish, the concept of parliamentary 'oversight' that drives the ISC.

The fourth Committee, appointed under Paul Murphy's chairmanship in 2005, not only faces the questions we have identified, but it must decide how it should change and adapt to meet future challenges. For all these reasons, then, and at such a crucial juncture in its history, it seems right to examine the role, responsibilities and activities of the ISC. Is it, like Bismarck's *Reichstag*, a mere 'fig leaf', in this case hiding the inability of the British Parliament to exercise genuine oversight of what the Agencies do? How does a comparative analysis of comparable oversight bodies inform our judgements about the effectiveness of the ISC? We consider these issues in some depth in subsequent sections, but conclude this introduction by summarizing our overall findings, which are set out in more detail in our two final chapters.

CONCLUSIONS AND RECOMMENDATIONS

As we shall demonstrate, the *primary* function of oversight in the US and UK is *not* to hunt down mythical 'rogue elephants' in the intelligence community. It is not there to seek out wrongdoing and ensure that the wrongdoers are suitably punished. That is not to say that an oversight body such as the ISC should ignore any irregularities it comes across, or that it may not, on occasion, decide actively to seek out such irregularities. And we accept that there may be other countries where intelligence agencies may be acting unlawfully or unethically and where oversight, if it is to be effective, will have a significant 'policeman' role to play.

Oversight is often seen as having as its primary (and negative) function the uncovering of misconduct. We maintain that this is wrong, and will argue that the basic rationale for accountability and oversight in liberal democracies needs to be fundamentally rethought. We make the case for an 'alternative rationale' that involves four positive criteria for oversight:

- 'Belt and braces': a quality-control mechanism reporting (in the UK) to the prime minister and Parliament, intended to support but not supplant the civil service's administrative mechanisms of control and constraint.
- **Standing instrument of inquiry**: a permanent, relatively transparent standing forum for ad hoc inquiries as the need arises, with the added legitimacy drawn from a composition of parliamentarians, rather than individuals appointed from the 'great and the good' external to the legislature.
- **Forum for the review of government intelligence policy**: a forum for review and, where necessary, challenge of the uses to which its political masters put the intelligence resources of a nation.
- 'Security blanket': finally, a means to make the intelligence community less (for some) disquietingly opaque and distant from the electorate and its representatives: essentially to provide a 'feel-good' factor for a population that has neither the time nor the resources to have an informed sense of the intelligence community, its abilities and limitations.

Bearing these four elements of the 'alternative rationale' in mind, we conclude that there are two key intelligence issues that the fourth Committee will need to address as a matter of priority: the continuing fallout from the Iraqi WMD fiasco, and the failure to anticipate the London terrorist attacks of 7 July and 21 July 2005. On the first, the main task of the ISC will be to ensure that the recommendations of the Butler Report are carried through and are having the desired results – indeed, to check that they are, in fact, proving to be the right changes to the UK intelligence system. On the second, the Committee should consider whether the Security Service and the UK intelligence community as a whole moved quickly enough to counter Muslim extremism when it was a subversive rather than a terrorist threat, and indeed whether the Security Service's definition of 'subversion' is too limited and has created a blind spot in its evaluation of threats to UK national security.

From this 'alternative rationale', and our analysis of the ISC's work to date, we conclude that there are other substantive intelligence issues that the ISC will need to address. But looking to the longer-term development of the Committee, in both this Parliament and the next, we believe that there are five basic issues that should be addressed by the prime minister, Parliament and the public:

- the ISC's status and responsibilities;
- the chairmanship and membership of the Committee;
- how the Committee conducts its business;
- how it is resourced; and
- how it communicates with Parliament and the public.

We shall contend that, in order to perform its 'alternative rationale' functions effectively and resolve these issues, the ISC should retain its present status as a committee of parliamentarians, however anomalous that may seem, but that it needs:

- the authority to oversee all the key elements of the UK intelligence community, including the DIS and JIC machinery, as well as government intelligence policies;
- a strong and experienced chairman, who should be drawn from one of the opposition parties;
- members with proven independence of mind and, ideally, some prior experience of intelligence matters;
- a strengthened in-house support team, with a clerk who works to a long-term strategy established by the Committee;
- a small panel of external experts who can be called upon to undertake investigations in specialist areas; and
- greater transparency in the exercise of its duties, with some evidence sessions held in public and fewer redactions to its

published reports; the Committee should consciously push the boundaries.

In making these recommendations we are conscious that there are contradictions built in to the ISC's position that cannot be reconciled; they can only be accommodated. We do not pretend that there are simple answers to these conundrums, but we do believe they merit informed debate. If there is one overarching criticism of the UK intelligence oversight system, it is that such a discussion has been largely absent in the past decade. We hope that this book may stimulate and contribute to the future debate.

1. The Regulation of Investigatory Powers Act 2000 (RIPA) further developed the parallel system of judicial review of intelligence with the creation of an Interception of Communications Commissioner, an Intelligence Services Commissioner, and an independent Investigatory Powers Tribunal. We do not consider these judicial elements in detail; a useful overview of them is provided on the Security Service website under 'Oversight and Legislation': www.mi5.gov.uk
2. 'Securing our Future'; address to the Royal United Services Institute (RUSI), 13 February 2006.
3. In this book we follow the convention that SIS, the Security Service and GCHQ are collectively known as 'the Agencies' (capitalized) with intelligence and security organizations in general referred to as 'agencies'.
4. Lord Butler of Brockwell, *Review of Intelligence on Weapons of Mass Destruction: Report of a Committee of Privy Counsellors*, HC 898, 14 July 2004 (London: TSO, 2004); hereafter known as the *Butler Report*.
5. Evidence to the Home Affairs Committee, 14 February 2006; quoted in the *Guardian*, 15 February 2006.
6. A short and not necessarily complete list of states that currently have intelligence oversight systems is: Argentina, Australia, Belgium, Canada, Croatia, Germany, Israel, Italy, the Netherlands, New Zealand, Norway, Poland, Romania, Slovakia, South Africa, South Korea, Sweden, the USA and the UK. They vary greatly in their responsibilities and effectiveness.
7. We have, in general, eschewed honorifics for simplicity's sake, unless the individual carried a title during the period under discussion. Thus, we refer to the Rt Hon The Lord King of Bridgwater CH PC as 'Tom King', but to 'Lord Howe' rather than 'Geoffrey Howe', as he was ennobled before appointment to the ISC.
8. See Sir Ian Blair, 'The Met is a Force to be Reckoned With', available at http://cms.met.police.uk/news/met_comment/the_met_is_a_force_to_be_reckoned_with_by_sir_ian_blair (15 June 2005).
9. The ISC is unlikely to probe into the circumstances that led armed police officers to kill an innocent Brazilian citizen, Jean Charles de Menezes, on 21 July 2005, as this is the subject of an inquiry by the Independent Police Complaints Commission.

10 *Iraq's Weapons of Mass Destruction: The Assessment of the British Government*, 24 September 2002.
11 There is no published figure for the totality of UK intelligence expenditure. The Single Intelligence Account shows planned expenditure of £1.361 billion by the three Agencies in 2005/06; to this must be added the costs of the DIS (published figures suggest these are in the region of £0.2 billion) and the comparatively minor expenditure on the Assessments Staff and JIC machinery. Gordon Brown has stated (RUSI speech, 13 February 2006) that by 2008 the UK will invest £2 billion a year in 'counter-terrorism and resilience' – twice what the UK did before 9/11. He did not provide details of what either sum comprised.
12 RUSI speech, 13 February 2006.
13 Percy Cradock, *In Pursuit of British Interests* (London: John Murray, 1997), pp. 42ff.
14 Quoted in Harold Shukman (ed.), *Agents for Change* (London: St Ermin's, 2000), p 68.
15 See: http://www.nao.org.uk/
16 While other parliamentary committees may see some classified material, only the ISC has potentially unlimited access to the most sensitive information.
17 'Notification that a person is subject to subsection (1) above shall be effected by a notice in writing served on him by a Minister of the Crown; and such a notice may be served if, in the Minister's opinion, the work undertaken by the person in question is or includes work connected with the security and intelligence services and its nature is such that the interests of national security require that he should be subject to the provisions of that subsection'; Official Secrets Act 1989, Section 1 (6).
18 ISC Annual Report 2002–03, Cm 5837; available at www.cabinetoffice.gov.uk/publications/reports/intelligence/intel.pdf (July 2002).
19 Developed Vetting provides an active in-depth examination of an individual's suitability to see highly sensitive material.
20 ISC Annual Report 2004–05, Cm 6510, April 2005, p. 4.
21 The interviews referred to throughout this book were held as follows: with Lord King of Bridgwater, first ISC chair, on 17 May 2005; with Sir David Omand on 14 September 2005; and with Lady Taylor of Bolton on 1 November 2005. All material quoted was given for the record and quotes used come only from these interviews, as approved by the interviewees. Information was also obtained in confidence from other senior former 'insiders'.
22 Cm 6510.
23 Cm 5837, p. 24.
24 ISC Annual Report 1997–98, Cm 4073, p. v.
25 *Ibid.*
26 At the Oxford Intelligence Group, 7 February 2005.

CHAPTER 2

DEVELOPMENT AND WORK OF THE COMMITTEE

THE UK INTELLIGENCE COMMUNITY: PLUS ÇA CHANGE...

Before looking at the genesis of the Intelligence and Security Committee, it is worth sketching out the development of the UK intelligence community (as it has become) over the past near-century. A useful overview is provided in the latest version of the Cabinet Office brochure *National Intelligence Machinery*,[1] which summarizes the background of the three intelligence and security Agencies. Of SIS it says, somewhat (but perhaps not surprisingly) unrevealingly:

> The Secret Intelligence Service (SIS), sometimes known as MI6, was set up in 1909 as the Foreign Section of the Secret Service Bureau under Naval Commander (later Sir) Mansfield Cumming. The Foreign Section was responsible for gathering intelligence overseas. It grew steadily and by 1922 had become a separate service with the title SIS. Cumming signed himself 'C'. His successors have done so ever since.

Of the Security Service:

> The Security Service, also known as MI5, was set up in 1909 as the internal arm of the Secret Service Bureau, under Army Captain (later Sir) Vernon Kell, tasked with countering German espionage. It became formally known as the Security Service (and theoretically stopped being called MI5) in 1931, when it assumed wider responsibility for assessing threats to national security, which included international communist subversion and, later, fascism. In 1952, in the early stages of the Cold War, the work of the Service and the responsibility of the Director General were defined in a Directive (commonly called the Maxwell Fyfe Directive) from the then Home Secretary. Many of the provisions were later incorporated in the Security Service Act 1989.

And of GCHQ (the Government Communications Headquarters):

> GCHQ was established in 1919 as the Government Code & Cypher School; it adopted its present name in 1946. Its successes during the Second World War (when its headquarters were at Bletchley Park) are now well known. GCHQ has two main missions: Signals Intelligence (Sigint) and Information Assurance. Sigint is derived from intercepting communications and other signals.

These three Agencies form the traditional core of the UK intelligence community, but there are two other main players: the Defence Intelligence Staff (DIS – recently renamed in snappy modern fashion simply 'Defence Intelligence') and the Joint Intelligence Committee (JIC). The DIS is described thus in *National Intelligence Machinery*:

> The DIS, part of the MoD and funded (separately from the Agencies) within Defence Votes, is another essential element of the national intelligence machinery. It was created in 1964 by the amalgamation of all three Armed Services' intelligence staffs and the civilian Joint Intelligence Bureau. The DIS conducts all-source intelligence analysis from both overt and covert sources. It provides intelligence assessments in support of policy-making, crisis management and the generation of military capability to the MoD, other government departments, military commands and deployed forces, as well as contributing to the work of the JIC. In addition to such assessments, the DIS collects intelligence in direct support of military operations, as well as in support of the operations of the Agencies... The DIS also provides a wide range of geo-spatial services, including mapping and charting, and a selection of intelligence-related training activities at the Defence College of Intelligence.

The JIC was founded in 1936 as a sub-committee of the chiefs of staff and reached maturity during World War II. In 1957 it moved to the Cabinet Office, where it has since been served by a dedicated Assessments Staff, which prepares draft intelligence assessments for the Committee to consider. *National Intelligence Machinery* describes it thus:

> The JIC is part of the Cabinet Office and is responsible for providing Ministers and senior officials with co-ordinated

inter-departmental intelligence assessments on a range of issues of immediate and long-term importance to national interests, primarily in the fields of security, defence and foreign affairs. The JIC periodically scrutinises the performance of the Agencies in meeting the collection requirements placed upon them...Its members are senior officials in FCO, MoD (including the Chief of Defence Intelligence), Home Office, Department of Trade and Industry, Treasury and Cabinet Office, the Heads of the three intelligence Agencies and the Chief of the Assessments Staff. Other Departments, such as the Department for International Development, attend as necessary.

The Foreign and Commonwealth Office (FCO) is often thought of as the sixth main intelligence player in Whitehall, even though it does not have a dedicated intelligence assessment unit. The foreign secretary is, however, responsible for SIS and GCHQ, authorizing their more sensitive intelligence operations, while the FCO as a whole, both at home and in its overseas missions, is a major consumer of intelligence.

...PLUS C'EST LA MÊME CHOSE

There have, of course, been many detailed developments within the UK intelligence community over the years, but it is striking how much has remained essentially unaltered. There have been structural changes, notably the incorporation of Military Survey, the Joint Air Reconnaissance Intelligence Centre (JARIC) and the Defence Intelligence and Security Centre (DISC) into the DIS. The first two of these then amalgamated, becoming what is now known as Defence Geospatial Intelligence, while the DISC is now known as the Defence College of Intelligence. The most recent significant development has been the creation of the Joint Terrorism Analysis Centre (JTAC), of which *National Intelligence Machinery* says:

> As part of the development of co-ordinated arrangements for handling and disseminating intelligence in response to the international terrorist threat, a new multi-agency unit, JTAC, was set up in June 2003. JTAC has established itself as an authoritative and effective mechanism for analysing all-source intelligence on the activities, intentions and capabilities of international terrorists who may threaten UK and allied interests worldwide. JTAC sets threat levels and issues timely threat warnings as well as more in-depth reports on trends,

terrorist networks and capabilities. It is staffed by members of the three Agencies, the DIS and representatives from other relevant departments including the Foreign and Commonwealth Office (FCO) and Home Office, and from the Police.

A further development was the establishment on 1 April 2006 of the Serious Organised Crime Agency (SOCA). This single agency brings together responsibilities formerly shared by the National Criminal Intelligence Service (NCIS), the National Crime Squad (NCS), and the investigative and intelligence elements of HM Revenue & Customs (formerly Customs & Excise) and the Immigration Service. In 2004 NCIS had 1,200 staff and an annual budget of £93 million, while NCS had 1,330 detectives, 420 support staff and an annual budget of £130 million. Revenue & Customs boasted a £1 billion annual budget and 1,850 officers in several different arms addressing fraud, drug trafficking and other cross-border crime.[2] In theory SOCA will allow a more 'joined-up' approach to fighting crime, but some people question whether its disparate elements will fuse effectively[3] and note the need to establish good relationships with UK police forces. The relationship between SOCA and the traditional UK intelligence community has also to be clarified; it would be appropriate for such a sizeable and powerful organization to have a permanent place on the JIC.

But, despite these novelties, the main core elements of the UK intelligence community have remained in place for over 40 years. Indeed, any World War II intelligence officer transported 65 years forward in time would find most of what he saw familiar. The lack of major change can be attributed, charitably, to the old saw: 'if it ain't broke, don't fix it'; or, less charitably, to a British reluctance to resolve problems through major organizational change, as epitomized in the US by the creation of the Department of Homeland Security following the terrorist attacks of 11 September 2001. British observers would no doubt cite the subsequent American experience as justifying the UK's more cautious approach.

THE ORIGINS OF THE INTELLIGENCE AND SECURITY COMMITTEE

Yet, despite the UK intelligence community's long and rich history, until April 1992 the UK intelligence landscape was, as far as the public were concerned, distinctly barren. The Security Service – MI5 – had long been acknowledged[4] and had been given statutory responsibilities under the Security Service Act 1989; the Ministry of Defence had always avowed the existence of the DIS, while the current existence of the JIC and Assessments Staff had been described in the 1982 Franks Report on the Falklands War.[5] Officially, that was pretty much it: there was no Secret Intelligence Service (SIS), even if every bus conductor shouted 'MI6 headquarters' at the bus stop outside Century House.[6] Nor were the intelligence collection activities of GCHQ acknowledged, even if it was one of Cheltenham's biggest employers. The government's stock response to parliamentary questions on intelligence matters was that it was not Her Majesty's Government's policy to comment on such matters – known to insiders as the 'neither confirm nor deny' line.

But in May 1992, then Prime Minister John Major owned up to the existence of SIS and GCHQ's intelligence activities, and in 1994 Parliament passed the Intelligence Services Act 1994 (ISA 1994), legitimizing and defining their roles, and establishing the Intelligence and Security Committee. What had led to this remarkable turnaround?

No one factor can be singled out as critical: rather a series of developments had made the official line less and less tenable. This process (or rot, as some maintained at the time) can be traced back to a series of 1970s publications on intelligence in World War II, beginning with J. C. Masterman's 1972 book *The Double-Cross System in the War of 1939–45*, which described the total success of the UK security authorities in rounding up and turning German agents, and which focused popular attention on the importance of intelligence. This was followed in 1974 by F. W. Winterbotham's *The Ultra Secret*, which revealed for the first time how important Sigint was to the Allies' success in World War II. Although criticized for historical inaccuracy (for example in claiming that Ultra provided forewarning of the bombing of Coventry) the book breached one of the last intelligence taboos – the fact that high-quality machine codes could be broken.

Official concern that works such as these would lead to a flood of more or less revealing (and indeed more or less accurate) accounts of wartime UK intelligence eventually led to the commissioning of a new series in the official histories of World War II, to be edited by Professor F. H. Hinsley: *British Intelligence in the Second World War*, whose five volumes (volume 3 being in two parts) appeared between 1979 and 1990. The UK intelligence community may have originally hoped that the appearance of this official history would draw a line under intelligence revelations and limit them to the wartime era; if so, they were to be disappointed.

The defection of H. A. R. 'Kim' Philby in 1963 had resulted in a number of publications providing details of post-war UK intelligence, but the most revealing (and authoritative) book to appear was arguably Geoffrey McDermott's 1973 *The New Diplomacy and its Apparatus*, which described in detail the role of the Joint Intelligence Committee (JIC) and the relationship between SIS and the Foreign and Commonwealth Office. McDermott had been Foreign Office advisor to SIS; here, for the first time, was an insider's near-contemporary account of the UK intelligence establishment and its workings. The failure to prevent McDermott from publishing opened the door to other books by UK insiders in the 1970s and 1980s, while US authors had never had any compunction about describing US/UK intelligence cooperation – a notable example being James Bamford's 1983 *The Puzzle Palace*, which focused on the National Security Agency (NSA) but described its relationship with intelligence allies, including GCHQ. By the mid-1980s any lay reader could obtain a coherent and up-to-date picture of post-war UK intelligence.

Yet right through Prime Minister Margaret Thatcher's administrations (1979–90) the government refused officially to admit the existence of MI6, or the intelligence functions of GCHQ. The situation had become absurd, and there may also have been concerns as to whether it was legally sustainable, given an increasing emphasis on human rights and the possibility of an aggrieved member of SIS or GCHQ making an appeal to the Court of Human Rights in Strasbourg. Be that as it may, Prime Minister John Major's government finally bit the bullet, and in 1994 the intelligence world changed, with the Intelligence and Security Act 1994 at long last regularizing the situation.

As has already been mentioned, the Act also established the Intelligence and Security Committee (ISC). It is important to note the responsibilities of the ISC and the limitations placed upon it, the relevant section of the Act being (the key points are summarized later for readers who do not wish to wade through the original text):

> **10.** (1) There shall be a Committee, to be known as the Intelligence and Security Committee and in this section referred to as 'the Committee', to examine the expenditure, administration and policy of:

(a) the Security Service;
(b) the Intelligence Service; and
(c) GCHQ.

(2) The Committee shall consist of nine members:
(a) who shall be drawn both from the members of the House of Commons and from the members of the House of Lords; and
(b) none of whom shall be a Minister of the Crown.

(3) The members of the Committee shall be appointed by the Prime Minister after consultation with the Leader of the Opposition, within the meaning of the [1975 c. 27.] Ministerial and other Salaries Act 1975; and one of those members shall be so appointed as Chairman of the Committee.

(4) Schedule 3 to this Act shall have effect with respect to the tenure of office of members of, the procedure of and other matters relating to, the Committee; and in that Schedule 'the Committee' has the same meaning as in this section.

(5) The Committee shall make an annual report on the discharge of their functions to the Prime Minister and may at any time report to him on any matter relating to the discharge of those functions.

(6) The Prime Minister shall lay before each House of Parliament a copy of each annual report made by the Committee under subsection (5) above together with a statement as to whether any matter has been excluded from that copy in pursuance of subsection below.

(7) If it appears to the Prime Minister, after consultation with the Committee, that the publication of any matter in a report would be prejudicial to the continued discharge of the functions of either of the Services or, as the case may be, GCHQ, the Prime Minister may exclude that matter from the copy of the report as laid before each House of Parliament.

The Committee's investigative powers were, however, limited by Schedule 3 of the Act:

3. (1) If the Director-General of the Security Service, the Chief of the Intelligence Service or the Director of GCHQ is asked by the Committee to disclose any information, then,

as to the whole or any part of the information which is sought, he shall either:
(a) arrange for it to be made available to the Committee subject to and in accordance with arrangements approved by the Secretary of State; or
(b) inform the Committee that it cannot be disclosed either:
(i) because it is sensitive information (as defined in paragraph 4 below [see following section]) which, in his opinion, should not be made available under paragraph (a) above; or
(ii) because the Secretary of State has determined that it should not be disclosed.

(2) The fact that any particular information is sensitive information shall not prevent its disclosure under sub-paragraph (1)(a) above if the Director-General, the Chief or the Director (as the case may require) considers it safe to disclose it.

(3) Information which has not been disclosed to the Committee on the ground specified in sub-paragraph (1)(b)(i) above shall be disclosed to them if the Secretary of State considers it desirable in the public interest.

(4) The Secretary of State shall not make a determination under sub-paragraph (1)(b)(ii) above with respect to any information on the grounds of national security alone and, subject to that, he shall not make such a determination unless the information appears to him to be of such a nature that, if he were requested to produce it before a Departmental Select Committee of the House of Commons, he would think it proper not to do so.

(5) The disclosure of information to the Committee in accordance with the preceding provisions of this paragraph shall be regarded for the purposes of the 1989 Act or, as the case may be, this Act as necessary for the proper discharge of the functions of the Security Service, the Intelligence Service or, as the case may require, GCHQ.

This is the Paragraph 4 of the Schedule referred to above, which defined 'sensitive information':

4. The following information is sensitive information for the purposes of paragraph 3 above:

(a) information which might lead to the identification of, or provide details of, sources of information, other assistance or operational methods available to the Security Service, the Intelligence Service or GCHQ;
(b) information about particular operations which have been, are being or are proposed to be undertaken in pursuance of any of the functions of those bodies; and
(c) information provided by, or by an agency of, the Government of a territory outside the United Kingdom where that Government does not consent to the disclosure of the information.

Thus, the 1994 Intelligence Services Act set out the parameters both determining and constraining the subsequent work of the ISC:

- The ISC was to be a unique committee of parliamentarians operating under statute and reporting to the prime minister. As such, it did not need to follow the conventions governing standing and select committees of Parliament.
- It operated within the 'ring of secrecy', with members cleared to see the most sensitive information, though not entitled to see *all* such information.
- It was required to provide an annual report to the prime minister.
- It could provide additional reports on any matter relating to the discharge of its functions.
- Sanitized versions of its annual reports would be laid before Parliament.[7]
- Its remit was to examine the 'expenditure, administration and policy' of SIS, the Security Service and GCHQ; it had no authority to obtain 'sensitive information' as defined in the Act.
- However, agency heads were free to disclose 'sensitive information' if they felt it safe to do so.

THE ISC DEVELOPS – AND BEGINS TO FLEX ITS MUSCLES

Though the nine members of the ISC were to be formally appointed by the prime minister, the process was, in practice, much the same as appointments to a select committee – that is to say, individuals were put forward by the party whips and appointed in roughly the same proportion as party membership in the House of Commons (see Table 1). Thus, the first Committee was made up of five Tories, three

Labour members and one Liberal Democrat; its chairman was the Tory Tom King, a former Northern Ireland and defence secretary, while the membership included another former Tory secretary of state, Lord Howe, and four other former ministers.

Following the Labour landslide of May 1997, a new Committee was appointed (as must happen after every election) with a dramatically reversed political make-up: six Labour, two Tory and again one Lib-Dem. Tom King, however, continued to serve as chairman of the second Committee until the 2001 election, which resulted in a third Committee with the same party make-up as its predecessor (though substantially changed membership) but a new chair in Ann Taylor, formerly a Labour chief whip. Two months after the May 2005 general election, the fourth Committee was appointed, chaired by Paul Murphy, a former secretary of state for Northern Ireland. Six of the fourth Committee were newcomers; one – James Arbuthnot – had served on the previous Committee, and two – Alan Beith and Michael Mates – had been members from the start.[8]

Even the ISC's most severe critics have never accused it of dividing on party lines; members have been seen to work as apolitical individuals, though some appear to have pursued personal concerns (as evidenced by the annual reports, with the stress on certain issues changing between Committees and apparently reflecting individual preoccupations). The reappointment of the Tory Tom King as chairman after the 1997 election appeared to send a signal that the ISC was above party politics, though the prime minister's 2001 choice of Ann Taylor as King's successor led to a few raised eyebrows. Some had hoped that the Liberal Democrat Alan Beith (a member of the Committee from the start) would be appointed in a continuing spirit of non-partisanship, and there were murmurings that Taylor was too loyal to the prime minister to criticize his administration forthrightly. In her interview with us, Ann Taylor robustly dismissed any such charges:

> I had been sacked by Tony Blair from the perfect job, why should I have been in his thrall?

In the event, critics could not find any explicit evidence in the ISC's reports that it was pulling its punches, though there are legitimate questions as to whether the Taylor-led Committee might not have been more robust in determining the limits of its inquiries. In this context, we look later at the differences between the ISC's

TABLE 1 ISC MEMBERSHIP: FIRST THREE COMMITTEES 1994–2005

	1994	1995	1996	1997 post-election	1998	1999	2000	2001 post-election	2002	2003	2004	2005
TORY												
	King (Chairman)			King (Chairman)				Arbuthnot				
	Howe		Blaker									
	Mates			Mates				Mates				
	Hamilton											
	Shaw											
LABOUR												
								Taylor (Chairman)				
	Gilbert			Archer				Archer				
	Jones			Jones				Howarth				
	Rogers			Rogers								
				Barron				Barron				
				Campbell-Savours				Strang				
				Cooper			Winterton	Quin				
LIB DEM												
	Beith			Beith				Beith				

examination of the intelligence on and assessments of Iraqi WMD and the later Butler Report.[9]

During its early years under Tom King, the ISC, as can be seen from its annual reports, steadily extended its effective oversight. It would take evidence from the Agencies on an area of intelligence, then ask their customers to appear before it to say what use they made of the product and whether it met their needs. This was hard for organizations such as the DIS to refuse (arguably impossible in the absence of a ministerial instruction to refuse cooperation), not least because of their importance as consumers of agency material. If the collection agencies existed to meet customer needs, it was surely necessary to seek customer views on the value of agency intelligence, for those customers to brief the ISC on how they went about their business, and then for the ISC to visit the customers' component elements to obtain further insight. Under Tom King, the Committee appears to have successfully inserted its foot in more and more doors and, without undue fuss, gently eased them open; as he put it more elegantly in his interview with us:

> The ISC is an incremental committee, in the sense that its remit has grown, has expanded to meet needs the ISC has identified.

By 2003 it seems to have been accepted that *de facto*, if not *de jure*, the Committee had effective oversight responsibility for the three Agencies, the DIS and the Cabinet Office intelligence machine (essentially the JIC and Assessments Staff).[10]

The development of the Committee illuminated a long-running issue. From the outset, some had argued (and still do) that the ISC should be a select committee reporting to Parliament rather than to the prime minister. Yet the issue of security has always proved a stumbling block. The argument went that, if any Committee investigating the Agencies were to operate effectively, it must do so within the 'ring of secrecy', untrammelled by security restrictions. Some of the issues to be examined could be so sensitive that any sanitized report would be worthless (this must have been the case for the 1996 ISC report – see below – whose subject matter has never been revealed). But if the ISC was instead a select committee, and its reports were not sanitized, to whom in Parliament could they be presented? Would there have to be a further group of parliamentarians (perhaps Privy Counsellors) outside the select committee yet within the 'ring of secrecy' who could read the unexpurgated reports, judge their worth, and report back to their colleagues? Infinite regression beckoned. As David Omand put it:

> They did debate long and hard as to whether the ISC should be another select committee and agreed that, even if they simply reported directly back to Parliament, the potential loss would outweigh the gain.

Nevertheless, the question has not gone away and we return to it later.

In the event, the ISC has obtained greater *de facto* powers than a select committee. In agreeing to look into the Mitrokhin Affair, Tom King laid down three key provisos, which the government accepted:

- Subject to the agreement of the individuals concerned, the Committee must have access to the papers of previous administrations.
- With the same proviso, it must be allowed to interview ministers in previous administrations.
- It must see policy advice to ministers.

These are freedoms that are denied to select committees, and, by successfully insisting on them before agreeing to undertake the Mitrokhin inquiry, Tom King staked out some unique privileges for the ISC.

THE COMMITTEE'S SUPPORT MACHINERY

Throughout its life, the ISC has had civil service support, described on the Committee's own web page as '…a Clerk and secretariat in the Cabinet Office'. The precise size of this team has not been officially revealed (though there appears no reason why it should not be), but what evidence there is suggests it is not substantial – in 1999 it appears to have comprised three full-time staff.[11] The secretariat team can be assumed to carry out the normal committee-support functions: managing the Committee's business, liaising with its interlocutors, maintaining its records, organizing evidence sessions and transcribing the results, briefing the chairman and Committee members before meetings, handling correspondence and organizing domestic and overseas visits, including personal support during the trip. From its inception, the Committee has travelled widely, typically visiting two or three overseas countries a year and making several domestic visits to agency headquarters and other intelligence-related establishments. Committee members have also participated in the biennial international conference of oversight bodies,[12] while the ISC has hosted a stream of visitors from foreign oversight organizations.

The Committee's support team has performed commendably, as successive reports in the first few years acknowledged, but the contrast with the very substantial in-house assistance available to the congressional intelligence committees in the US could not be starker. In particular, in the early days the ISC had to depend on written and verbal evidence from the Agencies and their customers, and, while members could ask any questions they wished, they had neither the time nor the resources to undertake proactive in-depth inquiries into specific topics. Recognizing this in its 1997–98 annual report, the Committee stated:

> [W]e are conscious that, in comparison to other countries, we lack the ability to investigate directly different aspects of the Agencies' activities, some of which have been highlighted in earlier Committee reports. We believe that enhancement of the present arrangements can be achieved without necessarily changing our remit or the law, at this stage, but by extending the Committee's reach with an additional investigative capacity. Such a person would need access to the Agencies' staff and papers, when required to meet the Committee's particular inquiry. We receive much helpful evidence from the Agency Heads and the staffs concerned, but we have not had the capability to conduct independent verification ourselves. Without such a capability, the Committee cannot make authoritative statements on certain issues. It would reinforce the authority of any findings that we make, and be an important element in establishing public confidence in the oversight system. This is important not just for oversight, but for the Agencies themselves and the public view of them. We believe that this is the right approach, and intend to introduce this capability in the coming year.[13]

Accordingly, the Committee appointed an Investigator, John Morrison, in 1999. Morrison (one of the authors of this book) was a former deputy chief of defence intelligence in the Defence Intelligence Staff[14] and as such had long experience of working with the Agencies but was not identified with any of them. Having taken early retirement from the civil service to become an independent advisor on intelligence and security issues, he was given a Cabinet Office contract to work for the ISC on a part-time basis as its Investigator. Over the following five and a half years, Morrison produced 14 reports for the Committee, on subjects ranging from broad and major issues, such as agency security, IT, R&D and people policies, to more detailed ones, such as secure communications, the Agencies' Joint Working Initiative, and how the functions carried out by inspectors general in other countries are discharged in the UK system.

The Investigator's work was praised by the Committee in successive reports, but in July 1999 Morrison's contract was terminated following his appearance on the BBC current affairs programme *Panorama*, during which he criticized the prime minister's use of the word 'threat' to describe Saddam Hussein's WMD capabilities. Although, at his request, *Panorama* made no mention of Morrison's work for the ISC, he was told that the Agencies had written formally to Sir David Omand, the Cabinet Office Security and Intelligence Co-ordinator, saying they had lost trust in the Committee's Investigator and could no longer work with him. We consider later the implications of this episode and what it says about the Committee's independence.

THE WORK OF THE COMMITTEE

All that the public officially knows about the work of the ISC comes from its published reports, together with the accompanying press conferences and annual parliamentary debate. This section does not consider their content, or what they tell us about the Committee – we address some of these key issues in Chapter 4. Here we merely describe what the ISC has done since 1994, as its reports are effectively its *raison d'être*.

The primary task of the ISC, as laid down in ISA 1994, is to provide an annual report to the prime minister. It has done so every year, normally around the middle of the year, though interim reports were provided in 1995 (soon after the Committee's establishment) and, in anticipation of a forthcoming general election, in 2000–01 and 2004–05. Sanitized versions of the published reports have been laid before Parliament (the redactions predictably coming in for media criticism) and subsequently debated in the House of Commons, though usually with minimal attendance by MPs.

In addition to the ISC's annual reports, the Committee has produced eight one-off reports on specific subjects:[15]

- *The Security Service and Organised Crime* (1995)
- (Undisclosed subject) (unpublished) (1996)
- Economic Well-being (unpublished) (1996)
- *Sierra Leone* (1999)
- *Mitrokhin Report* (2000)
- *Inquiry into Intelligence, Assessments and Advice prior to the Terrorist Bombings on Bali 12 October 2002* (2003)
- *Iraqi Weapons of Mass Destruction – Intelligence and Assessments* (2003)
- *Handling of Detainees by UK Intelligence Personnel in Afghanistan, Guantanamo Bay and Iraq* (2004)

With one exception, all these reports were produced on the Committee's own initiative.[16] That exception was the Mitrokhin Report, when the prime minister and the home secretary invited the ISC to examine the policies and procedures adopted by the security and intelligence Agencies for the handling of information supplied by Mr Mitrokhin, the former chief archivist of the KGB. The Committee has also produced a pamphlet on *Intelligence Oversight*[17] and maintains a website[18] that includes copies of its reports.

Every published ISC report has been followed by a government response. Until recently, these tended to seize upon any complimentary material, while rejecting or ignoring criticisms and requests to see material withheld from the Committee.[19] On seeing the government's response to the 2003 ISC report on Iraqi weapons of mass destruction, the Committee's patience finally snapped, and in its 2003–04 annual report it said:

> It [the Government response] emphasised only four key conclusions while either rejecting or failing to address fully many of our other conclusions and recommendations, which we regard as extremely unsatisfactory.[20]

A contrite government apologized in its response to the annual report and promised that henceforth it would explicitly address each of the conclusions and recommendations in the Committee's reports – as it did in that very response.

The Taylor-chaired ISC was dissolved in April 2005, prior to the 5 May general election; on 12 July Paul Murphy, previously a secretary of state for Northern Ireland, was formally named as the new chairman, along with the other Committee members,[21] though Tom King had previously argued publicly on the BBC *Today* current affairs programme against such an appointment,[22] maintaining that the ISC should be chaired by a parliamentarian from one of the opposition parties. Appearing on the same programme, however, Lord (Peter) Archer, an ISC member from 1997 to 2005, maintained that the ISC had always shown itself to be apolitical and had never split along party lines; this being the case, the party allegiance of the chairman was irrelevant. While accepting this, Tom King pointed out that the public needed to be convinced that the Committee was not susceptible to political influence, and that public confidence was undermined if the chairmanship was seen to be a consolation prize for an ex-Cabinet minister from the governing party. The leader of the Tory party, Michael Howard, subsequently wrote to the prime minister[23] asking that the chairmanship of the ISC should, as with the chair of the Public Accounts Committee, always be held by a member of the opposition. There is no public record of a reply from Tony Blair, and Murphy's appointment shows that the prime minister rejected the arguments of King and Howard.

We started this chapter by outlining the emergence of the UK Agencies from the shadows in the 1990s. By 2005 the process had continued to the point at which all three Agencies now have their own websites. The Security Service, bowing to the inevitable name it has inherited, bills itself as www.mi5.gov.uk. Meanwhile, GCHQ can be found at www.gchq.gov.uk.

Last in the publicity stakes, as usual, were SIS. But even they eventually provided a postal address (P.O. Box 1300, London SE1 1BD – not the Box 850 used as an internal government name[24]) and now have a website: www.sis.gov.uk.

We will return to issues such as the chairmanship later, but before doing so we must turn to the 'elephant in the corner of the room' – an issue that is clearly of fundamental importance but that so far has not been discussed. We are very conscious that so far we have implicitly assumed that oversight of the intelligence and security Agencies is both necessary and desirable – that it is 'a Good Thing'. To avoid such question-begging, the next chapter takes a fundamental look at the basic concept of intelligence oversight, and asks whether it is, in fact, needed in the UK context.

1. At the time of writing the link is: http://www.cabinetoffice.gov.uk/publications/reports/intelligence/NationalIntelligenceMachinery.pdf
2. *Guardian*, 9 February 2004, 'The Serious Organised Crime Agency: Q&A'.
3. A major problem in such amalgamations is often reconciling staff payments and conditions of service.
4. Lord Denning's report into the Profumo Affair of 1963 revealed publicly for the first time details of the Service's role and responsibilities.
5. Lord Franks, *Falkland Islands Review, Report of a Committee of Privy Counsellors* (London: HMSO, 1982). At the time there was a peculiar belief that it was acceptable to admit to the existence of British intelligence organizations in the past, but not in the present.
6. A peculiarly drab skyscraper now converted into luxury flats. When the SIS moved there, it had a petrol (US 'gas') filling station underneath the building. At some point it was recognized that this was not a very sensible idea for a potential terrorist target.
7. The ISC has also released sanitized versions of its ad hoc reports to Parliament, with the exception of two 1996 reports, one on an unnamed subject and the other on the Agencies' work in the area of economic well-being.
8. The full membership of the current Committee is:
Rt Hon Paul Murphy MP (chair)
Ben Chapman MP
George Howarth MP
Dari Taylor MP
Baroness Meta Ramsay of Cartvale
Rt Hon Michael Mates MP
Rt Hon James Arbuthnot MP
Richard Ottaway MP
Rt Hon Alan Beith MP
9. Two ISC members – Ann Taylor and Michael Mates – were members of the five-strong Butler inquiry.
10. Though, as we will see, there remained significant limitations on the ISC's ability to scrutinize the detailed workings of the DIS and JIC.
11. Select Committee on Home Affairs (third report, session 1998–99), *Accountability of the Security Service*, HC 291, footnote 27. Though not stated explicitly, these would appear to include the clerk. It may be assumed that, as elsewhere in the civil service, part-time staff are brought in to cope with peaks in support requirement.
12. The first of these took place in Australia in 1997, then in Canada (1999), London (2002) and the USA (2004).
13. ISC Annual Report 1997–98, Cm 4073, p. 25, para. 69.
14. The DIS is headed by a 3-star serving officer (Lieutenant-General or equivalent) who is the chief of defence intelligence, with a civilian (military 2-star equivalent) as his or her deputy. There is also a

military 2-star officer responsible for DIS collection and other non-analytical activities.
15 Some of these may be found on the ISC's website: http://www.cabinetoffice.gov.uk/intelligence/
16 There are no indications in the Committee's 1996 annual report that the report on an undisclosed subject was produced other than on its own initiative.
17 http://www.cabinetoffice.gov.uk/publications/reports/intelligence/intel.pdf
18 http://www.cabinetoffice.gov.uk/intelligence/
19 The Committee repeatedly asked to see the confidential annexes to the interception and intelligence services commissioners' annual reports; a request just as repeatedly rejected by the government.
20 ISC Annual Report 2003–04, Cm 6240, June 2004.
21 The delay between election and ISC appointments was significantly longer than on previous occasions; it is not known whether this reflected problems in recruiting parliamentarians to serve on an ISC that had received some bad publicity during the previous year.
22 Radio 4 *Today* interview, 7 June 2005.
23 *Guardian*, 10 June 2005.
24 SIS were traditionally known by various names: 'Box 850', 'Century House', 'The Friends', etc.; the Security Service as 'Box 500', 'Snuffbox' and so on; GCHQ as 'Cheltenham' or (only by outsiders) as 'Q'.

CHAPTER 3

IS INTELLIGENCE OVERSIGHT REALLY NECESSARY?

FIRST PRINCIPLES

So far we have looked only at the UK experience and the way Britain has grappled with the problem of intelligence oversight. But the ISC was not created in a vacuum: similar concerns have plagued other countries, and they have responded in more or less comparable fashion. But were their solutions any better than the UK's – indeed, is oversight anything more than a political fig leaf that hints at more than it is actually covering?

As already noted, the intelligence and security services were, for over 80 years, the quintessential *terra incognita* of British politics, subject to a sort of politically Wittgensteinian 'whereof we cannot speak we must pass over in silence'. However, in more recent decades, successive British governments found themselves roundly attacked for their endemic and persistent secrecy and secretiveness, portrayed as either laggardly or suffering from bad political conscience in their consistent refusal to consider mechanisms of independent or legislative oversight comparable to those established during the 1970s and 1980s by the American, Canadian and Australian governments. There was both chorus and consensus of criticism, with only a few commentators challenging the orthodoxy of transparency for intelligence.[1]

In a single bound in 1994, however, the UK government leapt past the Canadians and Australians, whose mechanisms of accountability had so often been held up by critics of the left as models to emulate.[2] Not merely did it place its foreign secret and signals intelligence services on a legislative footing (the equivalent Canadian legislation dealt only with the Canadian Security Intelligence Service), but it created a parliamentary oversight body (the Canadians had only independent review, and have only recently established a standing committee on intelligence and security). There can be no doubt that the ISC has subsequently had a palpable impact on the lives and work of practitioners in the intelligence community. Five years into the ISC's remit, MI5 Director General Sir Stephen Lander observed at a conference reviewing the Committee's first half decade that

> [i]t meets rather more often than sometimes I wish it did.
> It has been determinedly non-party political and discreet.
> We have felt the people are trustworthy and we can be honest and frank with them ... I think it's been inquisitorial rather than adversarial...[3]

And yet, despite providing a long-awaited response to chronic secrecy, parliamentary debates about the ISC's annual reports are poorly attended. The annual report itself may occasionally garner a headline or two, but little more. And while it may have drawn more attention on publicly debated issues like the lack of intelligence warning over the Bali bombing, inaccurate warning about Iraqi weapons of mass destruction, or mishandling of the intelligence community's public relations over the Mitrokhin Affair, these moments of prominence have been temporary and, in the case of Iraq, its deliberations and findings were quickly overshadowed by more powerful ad hoc reviews by Lords Hutton and Butler. Although it may work within the so-called 'ring of secrecy', its investigations have failed to reveal skeletons in closets, or unauthorized and inappropriate actions.

To be sure, the ISC fingered overspending on the 'doughnut', GCHQ's new head office,[4] and berated the intelligence community for a slow uptake on new information and communications technology. But, to be fair, government building programmes are chronically prone to lumbering overspend, and the civil service at large is notoriously incapable of managing large IT projects. On the whole, the actual findings of legislative oversight hardly seem to have justified the expectations of some. Indeed, with no obvious engineered coups or assassinations (successful or otherwise) by the secret services exploding onto the front pages of the newspapers (as they did in the US in the 1970s, prompting the creation of the current system of US legislative oversight), it could be argued that there was no immediate or compelling pressure to create the ISC in the first place. And, in many respects, its product seems to have been directly in proportion to its need.

Where the oversight systems in the United States and Canada were established on the back of public scandals, revelations and inquiries into *apparent* intelligence wrongdoing, there was no real equivalent in the British case. There was, of course, the fiasco of the Matrix Churchill trial[5] and the subsequent disclosures made by the judicial inquiry led by Lord Chief Justice Sir Richard Scott.[6] The ISC's first chair, Tom King, has recalled that the trial provided part of the impetus towards the drafting of the Act and the creation of the ISC,[7] but was hardly the major force. After all, during both the trial of Matrix Churchill Director General Peter Henderson and the subsequent Scott inquiry, there was no question of the British Secret Intelligence Service undertaking any unauthorized operations. Rather, duly authorized operations somehow had not quite been coordinated with investigations by HM Customs and Excise, with the result that, even before Alan Clark admitted in court to having been 'economical with the *actualité*', case officers from SIS and the Security Service (MI5) had appeared in court lauding the heroic virtues of the defendants, who had served as voluntary informants for the two services since as far back as the Cold War. A management failure there might have been, but not an intelligence failure; and, if there had been blunders or wrongdoings, it was Customs and Excise rather than the intelligence Agencies that emerged from the affair looking guilty. It is hard to see, therefore, where the political pressure might have come from for the creation of something like the ISC, not only as a new body, but as something that ran counter to decades of an unwavering UK government line on intelligence accountability and control.

Historically, the British government line, regardless of the partisan doctrine or ideological stripe of the government of the day, has been that the intelligence services are, and always have been, accountable to Parliament through ministers.[8] Even as enabling legislation was passed to regulate the interception of communications (the 1985 Interception of Communications Act or IOCA) and the work of the Security Service (the 1989 Security Service Act or SSA), the doctrine of accountability via ministers remained unchanged. In 1992, this led notably to a keen exchange between the parliamentary Home Affairs Select Committee (HAC) and then Home Secretary Kenneth Clarke. The HAC wanted to be able to speak to the recently appointed director general of MI5, Stella Rimington. Clarke rejected this claim on the grounds that it might set a precedent that could, eventually, make the Security Service responsible to the Home Affairs Committee rather than the secretary of state.[9]

But, as noted in the previous chapter, the defences against

openness had been crumbling for some time. By 1993 the administration of John Major had its Citizens' Charter and Open Government Initiative well under way, with unprecedented numbers of (pre-1945) intelligence files appearing in the Public Record Office and public avowal in Parliament of SIS and GCHQ's intelligence functions. There were private press briefings by the chief of SIS and the director of the national signals intelligence service GCHQ shortly thereafter (though SIS had always made sure that key newspaper editors were 'on side').[10] Yet, while the ISC was established and empowered to examine matters of administration, expenditure and 'policy', none of these had been in question during the Matrix Churchill trial or the Scott inquiry.

Nonetheless, while enabling legislation for SIS and GCHQ may have been a natural follow-on to IOCA and the SSA, the creation of a parliamentary Intelligence and Security Committee as part of the 1994 Intelligence Services Act was not. Indeed, the deep political motivations for the creation of the ISC remain unclear, apart from the fact that the existing natural candidates for oversight, the HAC for MI5 and the Foreign Affairs Committee for SIS and GCHQ, were not equipped to handle sensitive compartmented information.[11] There were, therefore, some economies of scale to be gained from clearing a single committee with dedicated facilities, set up to handle intelligence-related material. In many respects, the ISC seems to have been created almost as an afterthought, with a vague mandate, rather than being driven by any immediate, palpable political urgency.

As a result, for a decade the ISC has essentially been 'making it up as it goes along', in many respects finding a mandate or mandates for itself, rather than methodically fulfilling any clearly defined task laid upon it. And, after eleven years, we feel it is high time to pause, take stock of the situation, and assess how the ISC has reached where it is and where it ought to be going in its second decade. A natural point of departure is to deliberate in some detail on the first principles of legislative oversight. Why is it necessary at all, and what do we expect it to achieve? If we are to assess the ISC's work over this past decade, we need to have some measures and standards of performance against which to make that assessment, and upon which to make recommendations for the future.

HUNTING THE MYTHICAL ROGUE ELEPHANT

Frank Church's image of the 'rogue elephant' is the single most persistent idea that looms over the debate on intelligence oversight and control. The image of this creature took shape because of press reports about illegal activities by the Central Intelligence Agency (CIA) within the US or against American citizens, and the now notorious excesses of the Federal Bureau of Investigation (FBI) against civil rights and anti-war activists (and, indeed, almost anybody who incurred the wrath of its director, J. Edgar Hoover) during the early 1970s. As always, a US media feeding frenzy tended to affect the political perceptions of neighbouring and allied countries, and almost immediately the Canadians had their own round of rather tenuous scandals and a subsequent Royal Commission inquiring into the activities of the Royal Canadian Mounted Police Security Service (RCMP/SS).

Britain spent much of the subsequent decade or so suffering from various degrees of what can only be described as scandal envy, with the media and critics of the left falling with increasing desperation on the meagre scraps, ranging from chronic mole-hunting and unsubstantiated (and eventually withdrawn) claims that a cabal of intelligence officers might have plotted to overthrow Prime Minister Harold Wilson to the moralizing misrepresentations of Cathy Massiter, the embittered and frequently inaccurate reminiscences of Peter Wright, and absurd smear campaigns such as the notional murder by the 'security services' of anti-nuclear campaigner Hilda Murrell. Notwithstanding the seething partisan political desire to pillory national intelligence and security services for ideological reasons, virtually all the publicly renowned examples of 'rogue elephants' turned out later to be almost wholly mythical. As always, like the confessions of 'crop circle' hoaxers,[12] refutations and retractions in the intelligence sphere caused barely a ripple in the public awareness, compared to the froth created by the original accusations. The fact remains, however, that the piratical pachyderm is essentially a mythical creature, and that any oversight system established to seek out and detect it is established on erroneous premises and can only prove a liability rather than an asset.

This is not to say that there have been no covert actions to overthrow foreign governments, no wiretaps or intercepted mail. Nor is it to say that there have never been breaches of the law or propriety by intelligence agencies; but secrecy notwithstanding, intelligence services (as distinct from police services, which have a considerably patchier record) are no more likely to go awry than any other agency, public or private. Corruption, error and mismanagement are facts of human life, and are distributed more or less uniformly and consistently in various countries according to such things as legal system, institutionalized corruption, management culture, and so forth. Intelligence agencies are made up of human beings with human foibles. But, as a general rule, it is simply not the case that intelligence agencies act independently, according to their own or an imagined foreign policy, or violate the rule of law wholesale – and nor has it ever been.

One can take issue with whether or not the overthrow of Mohammed Mossadeq in Iran in 1953 was or was not a good idea; but neither the British SIS nor the American CIA acted independently when they mounted and executed the operation. For SIS, the requirement came from the Foreign Office, passed to SIS when the Foreign Office's own contacts proved inadequate to the task of toppling Mossadeq. Indeed, the operation (codenamed 'Boot' in the UK, 'Ajax' in America) was personally authorized by Winston Churchill on his return to office.[13] The US decision to participate was likewise an executive policy decision.[14] To be sure, both agencies agitated in some measure to have the requirement issued to them, and were in JIC and GCHQ alumnus Michael Herman's sense 'entrepreneurial',[15] in that they were willing to volunteer their capability and reassure policy-makers of their ability to perform the allotted task. But that is in no way equivalent to exceeding one's authority or acting illegally or against the wishes of the elected government.

The subsequent overthrow of Jacobo Arbenz in Guatemala by the CIA (Operation PBSUCCESS), on the back of the Iran success, was based on an explicit requirement for the action issued by the US Department of State,[16] as was the rather less successful attempt to assassinate Fidel Castro or topple him at the Bay of Pigs in Operation Zapata. In both cases, the fault lay not in the CIA making unauthorized actions – the Bay of Pigs action had been authorized by both the outgoing Eisenhower and the incoming Kennedy administrations[17] – but overconfidence in the potential for covert action in strongly established communist police states.[18] The same can be said of the efforts by the British, American, Belgian and Israeli agencies to topple Patrice Lumumba in the Congo – one senior UK official having described manipulating Congolese politics as akin to 'manipulating a blancmange'.[19] Here again, covert political action was not the work of rampaging parapolitical pachyderms, but operations mounted on the basis of tasking by national governments. Put bluntly, if one has a problem with operations Boot, PBSUCCESS or Zapata, one does not so much have a problem with SIS or the CIA as with the policy of figures like Ernest Bevin, Winston Churchill, Dwight Eisenhower or John F. Kennedy. To pursue the intelligence and security agencies over controversial operations is ultimately to bark up the wrong political tree.

As a result, the most commonly cited foreign intelligence 'excesses' become simply the covert side of overt national policy, in which the agencies are not so much freebooters as errand boys. The real questions that need to be asked about the errands in question have more to do with the taskmasters.

In the UK, we have no credible legacy of ostensible intelligence wrongdoing; nonetheless, the suspicion lingers that the UK government has harboured weakly controlled reactionary cowboys at the heart of the repressive state apparatus. In this respect, however, the government has rarely been its own best ally, trying as it has to shroud all intelligence activity in as opaque a cloak of secrecy as possible, as often as possible.

Perhaps the prime example of this is the so-called 'frogman incident'. In 1956 the British public and government found themselves confronted with a genuinely embarrassing 'loud flap' when an SIS domestic operation[20] was embarrassingly exposed in something approaching the worst possible circumstances. A diver called Lionel ('Buster') Crabb was put underneath the Soviet cruiser *Ordzhonikidze* while she was berthed in Portsmouth harbour during a state visit by Nikita Khrushchev and Nikolai Bulganin. Crabb was discovered by the crew, and the matter became the subject of an Exchange of Notes between the two governments – and an intense public furore. The government's response to questions asked in the Commons was a blanket refusal to comment on such matters. The operation had indeed been mounted by SIS, but in response to a requirement laid upon it by the Admiralty, which wanted photographs of the ship's hull below the waterline. The operation had also been authorized by the SIS Foreign Office advisor, or FOA. The FOA is a diplomat, attached to SIS HQ, who has the right to approve or block an operation, or refer the matter upwards to either the deputy secretary or permanent secretary of the Foreign Office, and thence even (via the permanent under secretary (PUS)) to the foreign secretary.[21] The unwillingness of the government to disclose these facts left a lingering impression of inadequate political control over SIS, and unaccountable freebooting by its officers.[22]

Lingering impressions like those brought about by the Crabb incident – regardless of how ill-informed they might have been – were reinforced during the 1970s and 1980s by the highly visible allegations and inquiries concerning intelligence in the United States and Canada. The result was a succession of authors, writing usually – but not always – from the political left,[23] determined to try and expose imagined American-style machinations and high jinks of 'unaccountable' British spies and their agencies, especially with the many allegations, insinuations and rumours about British intelligence that came into circulation at the time.

As in the US and Canadian cases, however, on closer inspection most of the supposed excesses of the intelligence Agencies in British history dissolve into misunderstanding and misrepresentation. It has long been acknowledged that Peter Wright, interviewed on *Panorama*, withdrew his claims that (mostly retired) intelligence officers had conspired to seek the overthrow of Prime Minister Harold Wilson – but only the claims survive in the popular, collective memory and the rhetoric of the press and the left. The retraction, more important by far, was overlooked or forgotten, perhaps because of its inconvenience. Indeed, Wright has much to answer for in polluting the public awareness of intelligence and how it works. Much as the retracted conspiracy remains in the public consciousness, so his (or, rather, Paul Greenglass's) artful phrase about MI5 'bugging and burgling' their way around London while 'bowler-hatted civil servants looked the other way' has lingered in the popular imagination, while his complaint that the head of the GPO Special Investigations Unit insisted on seeing a proper warrant before fulfilling MI5 requests for telephone taps is completely overlooked.[24]

Indeed, anyone who believes the issuance of warrants for communications taps is only a relatively recent phenomenon, postdating the 1985 Interception of Communications Act (IOCA) would do well to consult the 1957 Birkett Report.[25] That report articulated – nearly half a century ago – the terms under which a warrant would be approved for the interception of postal or telephone communications (the target must represent a 'major' threat in terms of espionage or subversion, and the intercept be of 'direct use' to the investigation that required it), and even provided figures for postal and telephone intercept warrants issued between 1937 and 1955.[26] No one was 'looking the other way' who should not have been, and those responsible for placing the taps were evidently attentive to both legality and propriety.

Much the same can be said about most other accusations against the intelligence and security services. Cathy Massiter's complaints about Security Service information being routed to an office in the Defence Staff (DS 19)[27] received considerable play in certain political quarters, but the idea that there could have been any moral ambiguity in using intelligence to counter Soviet subversion is at best absurd. The Soviet Union had a positive interest in the peace movement in the West, and went to considerable efforts to influence it. Much of that attempted influence was clandestine, implemented through what was then Service A of the KGB, and it would have been intensely difficult to monitor or interdict Soviet efforts at subversive influence and propaganda without input from the intelligence Agencies. And, of course, the idea that organizations like the Campaign for Nuclear Disarmament escaped KGB penetration and manipulation is as mythical as the rogue elephant.[28]

So also in the US case, where CIA domestic activities proved far less menacing than press reports originally suggested. When civil liberties campaigner Angus Mackenzie secured documents about CIA domestic activities through civil prosecutions and the Freedom of Information Act, what became apparent was that the great bulk of CIA activity took place abroad, and was intended only to investigate the extent of clandestine Soviet influence in the anti-war movement[29] (the same cannot be said of the FBI's interest). It is interesting to note that, on the CIA domestic activities front, the one thing that did breach the law was CIA receipt of intelligence reports on US citizens relevant to the agency's counter-intelligence investigations. Technically, this material should not have been received, or should have been discarded, under what has come to be known as 'the Wall' between foreign intelligence and domestic law enforcement – and, when it came to Islamic militants, it was precisely observance of this Wall that was to contribute significantly to the weak intelligence coordination prior to the 11 September 2001 attacks. The actions of the FBI and the CIA may have been formally illegal, but the law itself was fundamentally unsound.

Unfortunately, two crucial facts about the American intelligence scandals of the 1970s are typically forgotten. The first is that the American signals intelligence agency, the National Security Agency (NSA), so often demonized in cinema and other walks of the popular imagination, was the one national agency to escape from the Church, Pike and Rockefeller Commissions unscathed and with no wrongdoing to its name.[30] The other is that, having turned his inquiry into a media circus, Senator Church eventually confessed – once it was all over – that *he had not really found much in the way of rogue elephants at all*.[31] But that, like all the other retractions and published corrections, slipped from the collective public memory. The truth being ignored or forgotten, only the myth remained.

The story of inquiry and wrongdoing in Canada is similarly instructive. As in the United States, there was a series of press exposés of putative wrongdoing by the RCMP/SS. The public and political furore that resulted prompted the convening of the MacDonald Commission, which produced the 1981 'Royal Commission into Certain RCMP Activities and the Question of Governmental Knowledge'. During the inquiry, the government of Canada did not acknowledge having authorized the actions that prompted the inquiry, but it transpired in the years following that, within the terms of the existing procedures (established under the previous Mackenzie Commission in the 1960s), most of the operations undertaken had been properly approved.[32] It is significant that, where there had been inappropriate actions, these had been undertaken not by professional intelligence officers in the Security Service but by conventional RCMP police attached to the Quebec division of the service, G Branch. It was G Branch that ran unauthorized electronic surveillance and burned barns.[33] The punishment levied on the RCMP Security Service for its notional offences on the one hand, and its failure to control RCMP regulars acting in its name in Quebec on the other, was for it to be abolished and replaced by a new Canadian Security Intelligence Service (CSIS).

No sooner was CSIS established than its first director, Ted Finn, was dismissed for mishandling an affidavit applying for a warrant to intercept the communications of a suspect in the 1985 Air India bombing. The problem here was not one of misleading falsification, but a string of procedural errors that led to erroneous information being entered into the affidavit. The faulty information was not spotted by Finn, his deputy, or the Cabinet minister responsible – the solicitor general (who had to sign it off) – when the affidavit was approved. When the erroneous information came to light during the trial of the suspect,[34] Harjit Singh Atwal, the real scandal lay in the conduct not of the agency but of its political masters – of whom the journalist Richard Cleroux has observed

[t]he government needed a fall-guy. And they didn't want it to be the minister. The Conservatives [then in power] had lost enough cabinet ministers to scandals as it was...So it had to be Ted Finn, the Director of CSIS. Prime Minister Mulroney gave his approval and Solicitor General [*sic*] James Kelleher called Finn in and fired him...[35]

Despite the absence of any genuine rampaging pachyderms to be found in the governmental wilds of Canada, the UK or even the United States (where the spectre itself originated), two important lessons must be drawn from the futile hunt for this Loch Ness monster of politics. These are:

Given the excesses of the FBI, the heavy-handed tactics of the RCMP/SS's rank-and-file 'Mounties' of G Branch, and the succession of unsound prosecutions of alleged Irish terrorists in the UK during the 1980s, it is frankly Inspector Plod who is more likely to violate one's civil rights than the Spooks, and yet it is the Spooks who, quite irrationally, inspire most of the fear.[36]

If there are dark deeds afoot, from engineered coups to tapped telephones, it is usually politicians who are behind them and not what John le Carré has called 'senior espiocrats' (or junior ones for that matter).

And yet, strangely, the desire for oversight seems to linger, despite the main driving fear being based on what amounts to pervasive and persistent popular misconceptions about how intelligence and government *really* work. If one does start with a sound understanding of how such things actually function in practice, then it becomes even less apparent what role legislative oversight can really play in the effective management of national intelligence systems.

REAL CONTROL VERSUS IMAGINED

Intelligence costs money, manpower and other resources. To take as a point of departure the axiom that intelligence is not cost free is not as trivial as it sounds. The economics of intelligence remains an underdeveloped approach to the study of the subject,[37] but it is an essential approach for intelligence, just as it is for defence, health and other divisions of public policy. If we start with the assertion that intelligence *costs*, then immediately any discussion of intelligence activities, their oversight, control and management must acknowledge, and include in its deliberations, the role of certain key economic effects such as:

SUPPLY AND DEMAND Intelligence agencies do not appear *ex nihilo* but are established to serve a particular purpose and provide a product or service to the government that establishes them. In principle, agencies provide intelligence in exchange for a budget, and intelligence is therefore characterized by a form of *internal market* within government. Although this looks superficially like a monopoly supply situation, it is more complex. Intelligence agencies do not generally have discretionary control over the pricing of their goods and services; indeed, government both provides quotas *and* sets the price. So, although the three UK intelligence Agencies have multiple consumers, there is only one actual buyer, which is the Treasury. Hence, since intelligence agencies provide, at one level, a common product (secret intelligence, albeit from various sources), the internal market for intelligence is more akin to a *monopsony* than a monopoly, with a single buyer who has discretionary control over the price offered for intelligence goods and services. From the basic market-like characteristics of intelligence follow the next two considerations.

OPPORTUNITY COST Ordinarily, intelligence budgeting represents a 'fixed sum' game, in which assets available under the budget allocated to one task cannot be allocated to another. However, where the budget is already fully allocated (i.e. there are no significant surplus resources or *slack*), new tasks cannot be assigned or priorities altered without re-allocating resources from one function to another – at which point resourcing becomes *zero sum*. In either event, any given aspect of intelligence carries opportunity costs in terms of other elements of intelligence. Resources spent on Sigint cannot be spent on Humint or imagery – in other words, Sigint *costs* Humint and vice versa. And, as the SIS and Britain as a whole learned to their detriment over Iraq, allocating resources to collection *costs* resources that are not then allocated to validation and assessment.[38] Validation and assessment are not *direct* substitutes for collection, however, as they are appreciably less cost intensive relative to their *qualitative* contribution to the standard of intelligence that gets produced and disseminated.

COMPLEMENTARY/SUBSTITUTE COSTS OF ALTERNATIVE SOURCES
Different categories of intelligence sources serve at various points as both complementary and substitute goods. As a result, when intercepts of the *Abwehr*'s Enigma and hand-cipher communications with its agents in Britain (collectively codenamed ISOS) were decrypted in support of MI5 and SIS interdiction of German espionage efforts in the UK and abroad, Sigint served as a complementary good to Humint. By comparison, each year the government must decide how much of the Single Intelligence Account must go on each agency and its sources – at this point the Agencies are competitors for funds rather than collaborators, and their products serve as potential substitute goods for one another. This is particularly significant where the monopsony nature of the internal market for intelligence presents itself. Even if, or when, the intelligence Agencies choose to 'hang together' and act as oligopoly suppliers (as they tend to do in the UK, unlike in the United States, where the competition is more pronounced), their capacity to act as a pricing cartel is limited by the fact that they are always going to be in competition both with less cost-intensive overt sources of information, and (as with any element of public expenditure) with *non-intelligence* providers for the relative position of intelligence in public spending priorities, vying with, for example, healthcare or social services.

It is important to keep in mind that the age-old 'iron law of bureaucracy' – as Max Weber put it, bureaucracy is much easier to create than to destroy[39] – is something of a caricature, especially in the UK government. Richard Rose has argued compellingly that the post-war growth of the public sector has been driven chiefly by increased demand for goods and services (healthcare and welfare in Rose's reasoning, although this applies equally to Cold War security and counter-terrorism),[40] the implication being that, with an ebb in demand, public institutions can be cut back. Indeed, Andrew Dunsire's pioneering quantitative analysis of the expansion or otherwise of bureaucracy notes that there is as much evidence of the contraction, cut-back and reduction – destruction – of bureaucracy as of its enlargement.[41] The significance of this is that if departments, offices or agencies in government are not perceived by the Executive in general to be providing the services required of them, then they can be – and frequently are – shut down or dismantled, and their staff dismissed, released or reassigned to areas of increased demand.

It should be noted in passing that UK governments in recent years have sought to achieve reductions in bureaucracy via two main mechanisms. The first – epitomized by Margaret Thatcher's fundamental mistrust of the civil service – is to declare that the bureaucracy has become bloated and must be cut back. In her time, this was achieved less through direct staff reductions than by the transfer of functions – and the civil servants who provided them – to 'agencies' where, in ideological terms, the staff no longer formed part of the civil service and the organizations were somehow to be subjected to market forces. The second mechanism – applied in particular to sensitive areas where straight cuts would not play well with the public – was to reduce budgets and require the bodies concerned to achieve unspecified 'efficiencies' to maintain the level of service. In manpower-intensive areas, such as intelligence and security, this inevitably resulted in staff cuts, and usually also in structural change to 'flatten' the hierarchy and reduce the supposed top-hamper of senior management.

Intelligence in the UK government has long been characterized by demand-side constraints. This consumer-driven pressure has resulted in the regular abolition of intelligence machineries set up in war (e.g. during the various Napoleonic campaigns or in South Africa, or the post-1919 dismantling of the Directorate of Military Intelligence and its amalgamation with Military Operations in the War Office) once crisis expenditure no longer pertains, or if the political risks of a department's existence exceed the anticipated political benefits of its existence (e.g. the 1840 abolition of the mail-interception and code-breaking functions of the Post Office Special Section, or the dismantling of Basil Thompson's over-aggressive domestic Intelligence Directorate in the mid-1920s). During the interwar years of the twentieth century, the Secret Intelligence Service had its resources cut so far back that in 1935 the chief of service complained, now famously, that the entire foreign secret service budget was less than the cost of operating a single Royal Navy destroyer – in home waters.[42] Financial retrenchment in the 1970s forced SIS to reduce its staff across the board, resulting in whole directorates being abolished or scaled back, and its Latin American presence reduced from three stations to one – setting the scene for the failure to detect and prevent Argentine plans to invade the Falkland Islands.[43] After the Cold War, SIS was again pared back, with 25 per cent reductions across the board and ('flattening') a 40 per cent reduction in its senior management[44] – again creating the conditions for catastrophic failure, in this case in the Middle East and Iraq.[45]

In intelligence, perhaps more than in almost any other sphere of UK government, the internal market is primarily demand rather than supply driven. This inverts the standard expectation for governmental internal markets of supply-driven 'overproduction'. According to the overproduction model developed in the United States by William Niskanen, the nominal bilateral monopoly between political buyer and bureaucratic supplier favours the bureaucrat, who knows the actual cost of services and the actual volume required, but who exaggerates either or both in the pursuit of administrative empire-building. The result is an oversupply of public sector goods and services, driven by the supplier. In the UK intelligence system, however, the consumer demand dominates and often exceeds supply.[46]

Budgets and resourcing represent the single most effective and inescapable form of control for any government agency.[47] Even if the mythical rogue elephants of intelligence did exist, in most democratic governments they would quickly become sorry, critically malnourished creatures of more concern to their country's branch of the RSPCA or Humane Society than to civil liberties organizations. Even the vast US intelligence apparatus has been run to its effective limits (plus or minus structural inefficiencies and related costs on top of the basic operational, administrative and overhead costs of running intelligence agencies) virtually since its establishment. When the civil wars in Bosnia-Herzegovina, Rwanda and Burundi exploded in the mid-1990s, the US intelligence community – larger than the British by an order of magnitude – was completely unprepared, not merely from lack of foresight or interest regarding the problem areas in question *but because it was already fully committed elsewhere.*[48] Hard as it may seem to believe, overwhelming demand upon the finite resources of the US intelligence community figured centrally in the developing blind spots that led to 9/11 and the Iraq failure.[49] If America, with its vast expenditure, can still not cover everything it needs to know, what hope has frugal Britain?

The basic dynamic at work in intelligence resourcing is that countries develop and fund their intelligence systems in proportion to their strategic and policy needs. The United States needs global coverage because its interests are truly and comprehensively global.

Britain needs worldwide coverage because of its major power role, but it requires nothing like the depth and breadth of the US operations. Israeli operations may girdle the world, but they are focused in particular locations or are confined to particular problems that relate to threats to Israel, and never attempt the scale of US or British coverage. Meanwhile many other countries, such as Italy, concentrate on a high level of performance in their immediate locality; this effort they can then trade for a piece of the worldwide or global coverage maintained by their allies.[50]

The allocation of resources – financial, physical or whatever – to intelligence is in proportion to the need perceived by the *consumers* of intelligence, not the producers. If the Senate Appropriations Committee does not perceive a need for an intelligence programme, it will not get funded (and hence, like defence, intelligence expenditure is often the subject of much vigorous lobbying, especially by the Department of Defense (DoD), which controls 80 per cent of the national intelligence budget). Likewise, the size of the UK Single Intelligence Account reflects the priorities and primacy given to intelligence by the British Cabinet – and, constrained by official secrecy among other things, Britain's Agencies have less opportunity to lobby for their interests, although papers from the 1930s clearly show the War Office and Admiralty lobbying Sir Warren Fisher and his Treasury on behalf of the cash-strapped SIS.[51]

The ultimate point of all this is that the feed of any 'rogue elephants' is sustenance that must be redirected from other – legitimate and authorized – activities. Agents cost money; the hydrazine used to redirect a satellite into a new orbit is even more expensive, both in itself and because it is not replaceable in a satellite and thus shortens its operational lifespan; the appreciable manpower needed to sort through, evaluate and interpret intercepts likewise carries a very real expense. In other words, unauthorized activities carry very real opportunity costs for an agency that has to fulfil the requirements on which its budget is based. Operational funds spent on an illegitimate operation which, because it is unauthorized, cannot be factored into the agency's performance review and its business case for the funding levels in the next financial round, are objectively a waste of money. Obviously, the stricter the financial control, the greater the opportunity costs; but that kind of control requires a comprehensive set of requirements and priorities against which an agency's performance can be assessed. In these terms, the function of something like the UK's national intelligence requirements cycle has less to do with telling Agencies what to do on the grounds that they might not otherwise know, and rather more to do with creating an audit trail by which to assess the Agencies' use of their resources – an audit trail and specification of consumables agreed by, and explicit to, both sides.

It follows, therefore, that the most *effective* control architecture for intelligence must consist of three main elements:

1. REQUIREMENTS

A comprehensive set of national intelligence requirements and priorities, under which the intelligence goods and services being paid for by the public purse are set out as explicitly as possible.

2. BUDGETS AND RESOURCING

Although desirable, line-item budgeting[52] is difficult to apply strictly to intelligence, where expenditures cannot be planned in advance because targets and sources of opportunity may come out of the blue, such as 'walk-in' agents who volunteer their services without having been previously targeted and cultivated. One can, however, provide a contingency budget for unplanned opportunities that can be assigned in advance to allow some line-item provision for such eventualities.[53] Nevertheless, tying expenditure strictly to activities directed towards national requirements is essential, and maximizes the opportunity cost constraints on agency activity.

3. AUTHORIZATION AND APPROVAL

Operational approval may indeed have to take into account questions such as risk and consistency with national policy, but really effective control comes from testing any proposed operation against the national requirements it is supposed to fulfil. If operational expenses are tied to an approval process that takes as its first criterion the ability of an operation to fulfil one or more national requirements, then it is intensely difficult to undertake 'free enterprise', simply because the money needed to undertake it will not be forthcoming.

A system like that described provides maximum control in principle, and has, in practice, been used in the SIS for decades. The UK system is distinctive in the centrality of its national intelligence requirements process (NIRP).[54] In this system, there is an annual cycle, managed by the Security and Intelligence Co-ordinator, in which there is a dialogue between the government consumers, who issue what are essentially wish lists of information they desire, and the Agencies, which have to divide their resources across those wish lists. The resulting agreed system of national requirements and priorities is boiled down into the annual national intelligence requirements paper, and is coupled every five years to a long-term strategic review of those requirements.[55]

Michael Herman has argued that the NIRP is, at a certain level, superfluous because, in general, the Agencies and their masters will tend to have a pretty common view of whence and from whom threats that require secret intelligence knowledge originate at any given point in time. He has even pointed out that, for a while, the UK community functioned quite effectively without the NIRP to formally articulate its priorities.[56] In many respects, however, the real value of the requirements process lies not in telling agencies where to 'go and spy out the land', as if they would not otherwise know, but rather, as one senior SIS officer has put it, in providing a 'discipline' against which operational officers must be able to justify the costs and risks associated with a particular source or operation.[57] The NIRP provides something in the way of an agreed set of targets and standards, against which the activities and expenditures of the Agencies, their 'value for money', can in some degree be measured. It is, in other words, ultimately an *audit* tool.

Of course, no system is perfect, and the oral history of SIS is replete with examples of operational opportunities that were passed up because there was no requirement for the particular product at the time (a classic example often referred to by practitioners is a reported opportunity to penetrate the Eurocommunists early in the 1970s).[58] If, as Harry Ransom argued during the US intelligence scandals of the early 1970s, SIS – unlike the CIA – had never become a 'foreign policy boomerang' (of course, neither had the CIA, but this was far from apparent at the time Ransom was writing), it was because of the constraints provided by its requirements officers, who oversee the implementation of national requirements, and the Foreign Office advisor, who runs the rule over proposed operations before they are mounted or – if they are particularly sensitive – submitted to the foreign secretary for approval. Of course, it also helped that SIS has never been rich enough to spend money that did not go towards fulfilling national requirements.

Ironically, a similar situation lay behind the Iran-Contra scandal in the United States. Congressional refusal to fund covert support for anti-Sandinista resistance in Nicaragua led to Reagan administration officials trying to bypass the financial control and authorization machinery by using National Security Council staffers to do *sub rosa* what the CIA was no longer permitted to do by Congress. There are several lessons that might be drawn from the Iran-Contra example, one of which has been examined in the discussion of the 'rogue elephant' myth, and another of which (about excess control) will be examined below. But the main lesson to be drawn here is that financial constraints, and enforcement of a certain take on national intelligence priorities (i.e. that clandestine support for the Contras wasn't on the list, if there had been a list – which there wasn't), did effectively prevent the CIA from undertaking action of which some of its consumers (who controlled the purse strings) did not approve. To be sure, the administration tried to bypass that constraint, but it was forced to do so *outside* the bounds of the intelligence community. The intelligence community was indeed effectively controlled; the Executive wasn't. But that is an entirely different category of political problem, and is, in fact, the only really important one in the accountability debate.

There is an additional lesson that needs to be drawn from Iran-Contra: financial control (i.e. the Senate Appropriations Committee, in particular, and Congress as a whole) may have effectively constrained intelligence activity, but intelligence oversight (in the form of the House Permanent Select Committee on Intelligence (HPSCI) and the Senate Select Committee on Intelligence (SSCI)) completely failed to detect the subsequent private enterprise that took place.

In other words *legislative oversight cannot actually control intelligence* because it has no access to the internal workings of intelligence decision making and operations. More significantly, *if something is sufficiently clandestine to get under the radar of management and fiscal control, it is more than sufficiently clandestine to get under the radar of legislative or independent oversight*. Put bluntly, oversight does not and cannot imply control, and therefore oversight is completely incapable of preventing free enterprise and wrongdoing. It might conceivably provide a forum for investigation, and perhaps grievance or redress, but it can act only after the fact and once the damage is done. It might be argued that the risk of getting caught and investigated by an oversight body will constitute a disincentive to unauthorized activities, but firstly deterrence always has to be credible – how *really* likely is the oversight committee to catch miscreants at all? – and secondly, foreign human intelligence operators are specifically recruited because of a willingness and ability to try and get past the monitoring and oversight of heavy-duty professionals like the KGB or *Mukhabarat* organizations in the Arab world, infinitely more menacing adversaries than a part-time committee of otherwise fully occupied politicians. Even if there were improper deeds afoot – something that has already been shown to be relatively improbable – then legislative oversight is highly unlikely to detect them, simply because the information available will be incomplete (never mind the fact that those involved in the oversight would be pitting their wits against covert action professionals).

Another caveat about the oversight of intelligence can be drawn from economic theory – that is, what might be termed the *inverted U-curve of effective oversight*. The basic logic of this problem parallels the argument developed by neoliberal economist Arthur Laffer in his inverted U-curve of tax revenues. The Laffer Curve was essentially an inverted U-curve which argued that increasing the rate of taxation only increased revenue beneath a hypothetical threshold. Above that threshold, tax revenues would drop in proportion to the increase in taxation, as overtaxed earners lost the incentive to work at all, or began to evade taxes either legally or illegally, or took their business abroad to countries with milder taxation regimes, hence reducing the overall size of the economic pie available to be taxed. Laffer's hypothesis was, like so much economic theory, heuristic and more true in principle than in a real world where tax regimes can be tweaked, and where side incentives and allowances can be incorporated to offset the disincentives of the nominal tax burden. Likewise, if the burden of intelligence oversight becomes too heavy on either the agencies or their political masters, it will eventually become self-defeating. And, much as one can find evidence of the broad, heuristic accuracy of Laffer's warnings about taxation (the British economy prior to Margaret Thatcher's reforms is the most obvious example), so one can find ready evidence that over-regulation of intelligence actually undermines effective control of intelligence, either by creating prohibitive governance costs or by making effective action difficult or impossible, reducing the amount of intelligence that can be effectively provided on the national budget.

The classic example of this problem is the heavy-handed and often prohibitive role of the US congressional intelligence select committees in the authorization and implementation – or rather non-implementation – of covert political actions by the CIA. Unlike in the UK, Canada or Australia, the congressional committees are directly involved in operational approval for covert action. The basis for this lay in intelligence reform legislation passed in 1981, the last element of intelligence reform that followed on from the exposés and furores of the 1970s. As we have seen, of course, the problem of unauthorized covert action that this legislation was designed to resolve was almost completely notional, at least where foreign intelligence was concerned. Even before they were put into action, US congressional approval procedures were based on erroneous premises about how intelligence worked and what it did. Under the new legislation, the president was required to issue a 'Finding' requiring the covert action in question, and before the agency could go ahead with it the Finding then had to be – and still has to be – approved by Congress.[59]

The US system of operational oversight created three problems. The first was that it was leak-prone. The second was that it created additional procedural pressures, both managerial and operational. And finally, it introduced a glaring inconsistency, because no equivalent approval procedure was required for considerably more sanguine Department of Defense special operations. The porosity of the congressional oversight system revealed itself early on in the Reagan years, as congressional committee members hostile to the administration's covert action plans against Marxist Sandinista-run Nicaragua leaked details about those actions. Since then, however, procedures to detect and punish leakers have been considerably tightened up. On the other hand, the CIA has also learned a succession of hard lessons about the dangers of trying to get operations that have been tasked by the Executive approved by Congress, and the most persistent current criticism of the CIA's covert action efforts in the last decade was not that the agency exceeded its authority, but that it had been too risk averse, returning to the cautiousness and ineffectual passivity it had slipped into during and immediately following the inquiries of the 1970s, when it was under President Jimmy Carter's appointee, Stansfield Turner.[60] Risk aversion was a recurrent issue of debate during the 1990s, and has, of course, been a keen point of intelligence policy debate in the wake of the post-9/11 revelations about America's failure to get to grips with the long-term threat from Al Qaeda.[61] As a result, the US government has actually experienced a decrease in 'value for money' on a quite appreciable scale since it implemented congressional approval mechanisms for covert action.

The costs of congressional oversight should not have come as a surprise. Even apart from the flow-through nature of the congressional oversight committees, congressional control of the public purse strings was also being used to block a major feature of the covert action programme against Nicaragua: support for the counter-revolutionary 'Contras'. It was congressional financial intervention in intelligence that prompted members of the Reagan administration to bypass the conventional covert action machinery of the CIA and create an improved programme that funded the Contras with money gained from selling weapons to revolutionary Islamist Iran (sales also, futilely, aimed at securing the release of American hostages held by the Iranians). The ad hoc mechanism created functioned through National Security Council (NSC) staff (and not CIA, whose participation was confined to providing a single aeroplane used for secure transportation on a single occasion – additional requests from Oliver North and co. at NSC for operational resources were turned down)[62] and was essentially the covert action equivalent of tax evasion. It was the Laffer Curve of excess regulation at work, forcing people to act *outside* the regulatory framework, resulting in a loss of regulatory control rather than an increase.

Risk aversion and passivity are the intelligence equivalent of a prohibitive tax regime discouraging inward investment. Investors will simply not put their money into countries with prohibitively heavy tax burdens; this reduces the overall size of the economic pie and total taxable wealth, and thus cuts tax revenues. Likewise, an overly heavy intelligence regulatory regime discourages intelligence agencies from undertaking any but the most risk-free and politically anodyne operations in a sphere of strategic endeavour where initiative and boldness are at a premium. The result is a contraction of the overall intelligence product pie, with less to regulate because there is simply less significant activity and less benefit to be had from an intelligence capability.

To be sure, the then director general of MI5, Stephen Lander, publicly remarked in 2001 about ISC involvement in 'operational matters' that

> I have to say that concern about ISC's apparent lack of oversight of our operations is based on an illusion. If I had a pound for every time the Committee has asked me about operational matters, I'd be a rich man. And if you look down the reports

they have written there are quite a lot of operational issues: the Kosovo campaign, excise evasion, Mitrokhin, proliferation of weapons of mass destruction, events in Sierra Leone, and continuing risks from Irish terrorism. Those sound like operational not policy questions.[63]

But the kind of operational concerns referred to here are of a different order from the kind of real-time operational oversight and approval represented by the US model of legislative oversight. They also appear to reflect Lander's very broad interpretation of the word 'operational'. Most of what the ISC deals with is either after-the-fact review of specific functional areas of activity, looking at collection and analysis in broad terms, or expenditure and planning for operational or technological resources. Operational matters perhaps, but not *operations* as such. Indeed, the 1994 Intelligence Services Act allows the agency heads to withhold details of operations from the ISC, so it has no standing in this respect.

Even in terms of day-to-day routine activities, the US intelligence agencies (none more so than the CIA) have to maintain large legal and liaison staffs to handle their relations with the machinery of legislative oversight. Former Director of Central Intelligence James Woolsey is often quoted for his remark that not a single day had gone by when he had not had to go to Capitol Hill to testify before one committee or another,[64] and much the same observation has been made about his successor, George Tenet. The director of central intelligence (DCI) in America was historically responsible for coordinating the (now) fifteen agencies of the US intelligence community, as well as for directing the Central Intelligence Agency (the former 'community' function has now been hived off as the director of *national* intelligence (DNI)). It would seem plausible that he would have had more useful ways to spend his working hours in terms of intelligence management and production than testifying before congressional committees about activities he had so little time to spend upon. And much the same might be said of the considerable manpower costs of the liaison and legal staffs; how much *operational* manpower might the same budget allocation have bought? Oversight, therefore, is not an absolute good but is, at best, a question of *optimization*.

TRANSPARENCY AND POLITICIZATION

As two of us (Glees and Davies) argued in our previous volume on the Hutton inquiry, 'openness is not always a virtue and secrecy not always a vice'. There exists a widespread dogma that transparency is an unalloyed good, to be expanded wherever possible; and that it will, in fact, resolve any and all problems of public governance, as much in intelligence as elsewhere. As we argued at some length, the misuse of intelligence for public and parliamentary persuasion prior to the invasion of Iraq was a *direct consequence of excessive and ill-considered openness*. Essential to our argument then was the idea that moving intelligence into the public spotlight inherently politicizes it and turns it into a 'political football'; it can no longer assess its information and make its judgements independently, but must increasingly be seen to toe a party line.[65] The idea of legislative oversight can be seen as both a reflection of that blind orthodoxy, and potentially an arena in which the political football of intelligence is put into play – and where it is potentially most likely to be kicked around for partisan purposes.

We have already seen how partisan political leaking took place in the US congressional intelligence committee system during the 1980s. While leaks may now be rarer, the evidence from the American inquiries into Iraq is that the tendency towards partisanship has, if anything, intensified since 2001. This is perhaps most depressingly apparent in the 2004 review of pre-war intelligence assessments of Iraqi WMD programmes conducted by the Senate Select Committee on Intelligence. Between the actual invasion of Iraq and the production of the report by the SSCI there had been off-year congressional elections that shifted the US Senate from a slim Democrat majority to a slim Republican one. Furthermore, the report was to be published in a presidential election year by a committee that had the election outcomes at least in the back of its mind – and a Democrat presidential hopeful (John Edwards) as the ranking Democrat on it.

The resulting report was what one of the present authors (Philip Davies) has described as a 'bipartisan partisan' document, in which members from both parties needed to find a scapegoat for the decision to go to war – the Republicans to protect the chances of the Republican incumbent George W. Bush seeking re-election, and the Democrats to distance themselves from the fact that all but two of them (including then SSCI Chairman Bob Graham) had voted for a war they now wanted to oppose in the election campaign. The result was that any shred of independence in the legislative review was completely lost, and the value of legislative oversight in this matter was utterly negated.

In the British case, there is a very real risk that creating a permanent body that calls civil servants of any stripe (intelligence or otherwise) to account runs the risk of creating a permanent armature to allow ministers to perform what might be called the 'Aberfan manoeuvre' – avoiding responsibility for their actions by deflecting blame onto their civil servants.[66] And the Aberfan manoeuvre has been used in the intelligence context – the classic British example being governmental denial of the 'Buster' Crabb frogman incident of 1956, an operational requirement properly laid upon SIS by the Admiralty, and duly approved by the Foreign Office. In response, the Eden government denied knowledge and responsibility, promoted the Foreign Office official who approved action 'sideways' out of the approval role, and, most significantly, dismissed the serving chief of the SIS, Sir John Sinclair.

It is with experiences like this in mind that one is not surprised to learn that much of the impetus for intelligence legislation came from the Agencies themselves – keen to avoid such a situation in the case of a public 'loud flap' over future blown operations.[67] In the British system, sensitive operations must be authorized by ministers, and the continued availability of the warrants for inspection by the appropriate commissioner[68] constitutes a far more effective check on attempts to dodge ministerial responsibility than any external oversight committee, and one with far greater independence. As a result, parliamentary intelligence oversight actually constitutes a positive threat to ministerial accountability – but in a way profoundly different from that which concerned Home Office officials and Ken Clarke in 1992.

The temptation to engage in the Aberfan manoeuvre also, more than ever, invites the divisive pressures of partisan political interest into the Committee. Government members may wish to use the Committee to exonerate ministers from responsibility, especially if they are parliamentarians whose careers are still in flux and who may be beholden to the government of the day for future appointments and portfolios. Or there may be a passive lack of impetus to ask the right questions, a failure to choose the right subject for inquiry or to be sufficiently incisive and critical. This is particularly a risk where members of the Committee may be at a point in their political career where they still have hope of preferment. It is the chair's responsibility to ensure the ISC's independence from political pressure, and all the chairs to date have been – or appeared to be – at the end of their political careers. But the calibre of the chairman is important; the ISC's first chair, Tom King, might have been a senior former Cabinet minister, experienced in security and intelligence affairs and nearing the end of a long and illustrious political career, but the same could not be said of the second or third incumbents. The current conduct of the Blair administration has also made it profoundly unlikely that they would ever choose a chair with either the gravitas or *independence* of Lord King, regardless of party stripe (a matter to which this discussion will turn again in due course).

Legislative oversight is not, therefore, likely to prevent the occurrence of rogue actions – which are not really very likely in the first place. Nor can it provide a credible dual-channel apparatus of direction and control, as it will always – at best – be on the outside looking in. And even if one could, and did, try to implement legislative oversight as just such a control channel, it would in all likelihood prove counter-productive and ultimately self-defeating, as the US model has arguably proved to be.

What credible role can be found, therefore, for the legislative oversight of intelligence?

ALTERNATIVE PARADIGMS FOR ACCOUNTABILITY

Stated bluntly, the commonly accepted grounds, justifications and purposes for intelligence oversight are, for the most part, simply wrong. The 'rogue elephant' is a myth, at least where intelligence proper is concerned, and oversight bodies are inherently unable to provide the kind of constraint and control that critics of the intelligence community so often appear to want to see. It is also evident that really effective day-to-day control and constraint lie in rigorous governmental mechanisms of direction and authorization, rather than in any outside, retrofitted and jury-rigged auxiliary mechanism. What role, therefore, is left to any legislative entity 'overseeing' intelligence?

Ultimately, there are only four credible intelligence oversight functions in any government:

1. 'Belt and braces'
2. Standing instrument of inquiry
3. Executive intelligence policy review forum
4. 'Security blanket'

'BELT AND BRACES' No mechanism of administrative control is fault free, and neither are its human participants; so a back-up mechanism of inspection and quality control is only sensible. Intelligence officials are as fallible as anyone else, both practically and ethically, and there is a sound case to be made for an oversight mechanism whose function is to ensure the effective implementation, operation and observance of the administrative controls described above. This dovetails with a long-standing argument against the 'rogue elephant' consensus made by a number of key commentators.[69] That argument is that intelligence oversight should not be about operational constraint but, rather, that it should inspect and ensure 'value for money' from the intelligence system. However, the case for legislative oversight as a mechanism of inspection, and for quality control as a check on 'value for money', is subject to the same objection as legislative oversight as a back-up managerial structure. It is external to the administration of intelligence, and any financial mismanagement that can slip below the horizon of administrative control will also be below the horizon of legislative surveillance. As a result, it is very likely that, were an organization to go awry (more in the sense of mismanagement or institutionalized error than unauthorized action), it is highly unlikely that an external oversight body could detect or prevent this *at the time*, though it may well pick it up after the event as the chickens come home to roost.[70]

There are two further crucial objections to the 'value for money' argument, both of which hinge upon the essentially amateur nature of a committee of parliamentarians, few of whom will have the insider's knowledge of the inner workings and arcana of intelligence. The first is a return to Niskanen's overproduction hypothesis, i.e. that bureaucrats, having a first-hand understanding of the real costs and needs for the goods and services their departments provide, are in a position to exaggerate that need and convince their political consumers and paymasters to waste money on the 'overproduction' of those goods and services.[71] Michael Herman has observed that this is a particular risk with large-scale, technical intelligence producers, whose methods are more likely to escape the understanding of less technologically adept political folk.[72] Whether it is or not, the problem is that the legislative committee member is forever in danger of being 'blinded by science' and, as a 'dilettante' (to use the expression of Max Weber) in the technically complex affairs of state, is likely to be ill-equipped to test and challenge the assertions of the professionals (a hazard hardly unique to intelligence). The other risk, noted by Ken Robertson on the creation of the ISC, is that, with initiation into the inner workings of intelligence, the Committee could become a constituency for, and voice on behalf of, the intelligence community.[73] Its members might, in Jonathan Lynn and Antony Jay's sense, 'go native'[74] and cease to be an effective check on anyone or anything at all.

On the other hand, even the most limited external review can be a valuable check on the tendency of any organization to take on 'the characteristics of a coterie'[75] or become mired in an unreflective and unchallenged 'closed society'.[76] Likewise, any kind of control, administrative or otherwise, can be imagined as something like a polarized filter. Some things that slip through because of the orientation of one filter might get caught by a second filter with a different orientation – however, this does verge on sending one's oversight body on an ill-defined fishing trip, more dependent on serendipity than mandate. If one does judge such a limited second filter to be cost effective, then legislative oversight, like independent oversight (in the Canadian model of the Security Intelligence Review Committee), is as good a means as any.

Both the risks of the domineering bureaucrat and the overseer going native can be mitigated to a large extent by institutional experience and having members of the legislative oversight body who are sufficiently qualified. Over time, a permanent entity acquires a very real body of institutional experience and know-how, especially when there is a rotation or continuity of members of the committee, rather than having a completely clean sweep of new appointees.[77] The benefits of that institutional experience can be seen both in the first half decade of the ISC's work, and in something like the joint congressional inquiry into the terrorist attacks, which successfully brought the collective understanding and know-how of both the House and Senate intelligence committees to bear, and in a truly bipartisan fashion.[78] Both of these advantages can, of course, be done away with in favour of partisan manipulation if the government of the day simply appoints a completely new Committee each time round, or appoints a membership over which it has substantial influence, explicit or tacit. But if a government can resist the urge to staff the Committee with placemen, lackeys and flunkies, it can acquire its own independent credibility and political clout within Whitehall.

STANDING INSTRUMENT OF INQUIRY Investigations into various flaps and scandals that have involved intelligence and the intelligence and security Agencies have been characterized by an assortment of different investigative mechanisms. A persistent problem of credibility and legitimacy in UK intelligence policy has been that of the lack of viable or credible channels through which individuals may bring grievances against the intelligence community if error or misconduct may have occurred. Secrecy and the rules of evidence in the UK have historically made it difficult for citizens to bring civil suits against intelligence and security services, as has been done on occasion in the United States.[79] In the UK, ever since IOCA, the main conduit for grievances have been Tribunal and commissioner, established under IOCA and reinforced by the 1989 Security Service Act; both of these operate within the 'ring of secrecy' and both keep their evidence and deliberations secret. The lack of findings against the Agencies has done little to convince observers (or complainants) that there have genuinely been no errors or wrongdoing.[80] Inadequate transparency has always robbed the commissioner and Tribunal of a degree of public legitimacy and credibility. By the same token, Security Commission inquiries from the 1960s to the 1980s, and inquiries by Privy Counsellors such as Lord Franks, have had to tread carefully to avoid revealing sensitive information, and to that extent they have failed to convince a sceptical public.

Even when inquiries have been as open as Scott, Hutton and Butler, only the Butler inquiry had a starting familiarity with intelligence issues, and an appreciable proportion of the others' deliberation time was taken up simply learning about the subject matter. This is another case of opportunity costs, in this case when time spent learning the ropes would have been better spent investigating them, had the inquiry body had a corpus of knowledge and a precedent of access already in place. There is, therefore, a strong case to be made for a parliamentary forum for post hoc inquiry into mistakes, wrongdoings and other problems that could systematically and consistently hold the Agencies and officials (and, as will be argued in a moment, ministers) to account. Here again there are risks of dilettantism and of members going native but, like the 'belt and braces' case, these can be mitigated by appropriate membership, permanence and collective experience.

EXECUTIVE INTELLIGENCE POLICY REVIEW FORUM As was observed at the outset, the traditional UK approach to the accountability of intelligence was that the intelligence Agencies were accountable to Parliament via ministers holding seats in Parliament and answering to Parliament. The constitutional (if it can be called that) basis for this view has been examined chiefly from the point of view of whether ministers can indeed provide direction and control. The answer is that, in most cases, they can – provided there is stringent financial control, a rigorous operational clearance process, and a clearly articulated set of requirements to which the operational Agencies can be held to account. That is, they can be expected to ensure that the Agencies act in accordance with national policy and the law – in the sense that the law provides for terms and conditions under which it can be abrogated by the Agencies with appropriate warrants and authorizations.

To look at the often misdirected flaps and furores about intelligence getting out of control, however, the essential issue has not been that SIS, the CIA or anyone else exceeded their briefs in Iran, Guatemala, the Congo, Cuba or Chile. The problem is that, once the activities emerged into the glare of publicity, observers, commentators and often legislators themselves have fundamentally *disagreed* with those actions, whether or not they were authorized. As has already been argued, the problem lay not with the Agencies, but with their political masters; and in many respects that is the natural and most useful place for any *legislative* mechanism of accountability and oversight of intelligence to rest. It lies not with the Agencies and their management but with the policies and requirements laid upon them by government.

It can, however, be quite plausibly argued that, in the contemporary British system, the Cabinet has become *de facto* the Crown. Such a conclusion rejects the traditional constitutional notion of Cabinet as fulfilling parliamentary oversight of the executive machinery of the Crown; in which case, the role of oversight changes dramatically. Just such a transformation is implicit in the creation, during the 1980s, of the system of parliamentary select committees. Rather than being an oversight body, Parliament has become the Crown entity that itself needs to be overseen.[81] From this perspective it is not enough to say that operations Boot, PBSUCCESS or Zapata were properly authorized and consistent with national policy *if one believes that there needs to be a real-time, concurrent check on that national policy*. If governments – that is *administrations* – are authorizing actions the legislature finds objectionable, then there is a case for legislative oversight of activities where this is a risk.

In many respects, this was the real crux of the matter when

Congress blocked the funds for the Contras, or when individual Congressmen leaked details about mining Nicaragua's harbours. The real problem was not that intelligence agencies were doing these things, but that the Reagan administration was requiring them to do so. It was a misplaced concern about agencies rather than politicians that contributed to the late realization that, when push came to shove, the politicians could completely bypass the national agencies in order to bypass congressional oversight. Congress took its eye off the ball. Even if administrations are not authorizing questionable actions, there exists the possibility that they may be making unsound and ill-considered decisions about national requirements and priorities – and perhaps even that they are not authorizing robust actions when they should. If one no longer accepts that ministers should be left to themselves to manage the affairs of state – and on the whole they probably should not – then the inescapable conclusion is that the *real function* of the legislative oversight should ultimately be *to monitor the executive use of intelligence agencies* rather than the Agencies themselves. It is, to say the least, doubtful that ISA 1994, in requiring the ISC to examine the 'policy' of the Agencies, intended the Committee to work up the line to examine the government policies that ultimately direct the Agencies' work – but one might legitimately ask 'why not?'

'SECURITY BLANKET' People have a natural distrust of secret organizations, and there are influential and vocal civil libertarian ideological groups (of both left and right) who have a great capacity to undermine good governance in the name of absolute freedom. A major function of legislative oversight is not, therefore, to actually *oversee* anything, but to be *seen to oversee* intelligence – laying public fears to rest, defusing the challenges from ideological groups, and generally trading institutional window-dressing for improved popular legitimacy.[82] Like science policy, intelligence is a field that the general public is ill-equipped to understand and effectively discuss, and, like science policy, good work can be undermined by the agitation of sententious political ideologues.[83]

The machinery of transparency then becomes about making a show of laying fears to rest and providing the electorate and dubious legislators with a kind of political 'security blanket' intended, ultimately, to make the intelligence community non-threatening to the uninformed observer. Such a justification reduces legislative oversight to little more than formal compliance on the one hand, and perception management (i.e. spin-doctoring) on the other. These are real political functions and, in terms of political practicality, sensible justifications for the *utility* of an oversight body, regardless of its actual effectiveness in doing oversight. Whether this is the counsel of hard-nosed realism or of despair, it is a possibility that must be examined carefully because, even if an oversight body does not start out as such a thing, it may end up so.

What any country must decide is which – or which combination – of these realistic intelligence oversight functions any intelligence oversight body is intended to perform. In the UK, we have been unwilling to be explicit about them, perhaps simply as a consensus-building strategy of allowing the ISC to appear 'all things to all men'. But after a decade, this is an attitude that the UK can no longer afford, especially after the complete failure of the ISC to grasp the nettle over crucial matters such as the intelligence on Iraqi weapons of mass destruction, or the government's desire to use intelligence for public persuasion. It is time for us to be clear-minded and realistic as to the functions we give any body like the ISC, and as to what we actually can and should expect it to achieve. To what degree has the ISC fallen into the traps and by-ways that have misdirected experiments with oversight in other countries, and to what degree has it charted its own course? And, considering the calmer and more methodical political climate in which it was created – compared with the Canadian and American systems – to what degree has the Committee anticipated and embodied aspects of the 'alternative' model of oversight developed here? To assess these questions, and the overall success of the ISC as a project, we need to examine its evolution and work since 1994.

1   Perhaps the leading voice of dissent throughout the 1980s and 1990s was Kenneth Gordon (K. G.) Robertson; see, for example, his *Public Secrets* (London: Macmillan, 1984).
2   See, for example, Peter Gill, *Policing Politics* (London: Frank Cass, 1994) or Iain Leigh and Lawrence Lustgarten, *In from the Cold: National Security and Parliamentary Democracy* (Oxford: Clarendon Press, 1994).
3   Stephen Lander, 'The Oversight of Security and Intelligence', presented to the Security and Intelligence Studies Group and Royal United Services Institute joint conference on a five-year review of the ISC's activity in 2001, p. 5.

4   In fact, the National Audit Office fingered this particular matter well before the ISC, and with more direct access to the expenditure information.
5   Various different accounts of the Matrix Churchill, and the related Ordtech, trials can be found variously in Mark Phythian, *Arming Iraq* (Boston: Northeastern University Press, 1997); Davina Miller, *Export or Die: Britain's Defence Trade with Iran and Iraq* (London: Cassell, 1996); David Leigh, *Betrayed: The Real Story of the Matrix Churchill Trial* (London: Bloomsbury, 1993); Richard Norton-Taylor, *The Truth is a Difficult Concept: Inside the Scott Inquiry* (London: Fourth Estate, 1995); and Chris Cowley, *Guns, Lies and Spies: How We Armed Iraq* (London: Hamish Hamilton, 1992).
6   Richard Scott, *Report of the Inquiry into the Export of Defence Equipment and Dual-Use Goods to Iraq and Related Prosecutions* (London: HMSO, 1996), 5 volumes + Index and CD-Rom.
7   Interview with A. Glees and P. H. J. Davies.
8   Harold Wilson, *The Governance of Britain* (London: Weidenfeld & Nicolson, 1976), pp. 167–68; K. G. Robertson, 'Accountable Intelligence: The British Experience', *Conflict Quarterly*, Vol. 8, No. 1 (winter 1988), *passim*.
9   Parliamentary Home Affairs Committee, *Accountability of the Security Service: First Report of the Home Affairs Committee*, HC265 (London: HMSO, 1992). It is worth noting, however, that after the row limited arrangements were made for a small group of MPs, including HAC members, to meet with the DG.
10 For a detailed discussion of the Open Government Initiative, and its potential for the politicization of intelligence, see Anthony Glees and Philip Davies, *Spinning the Spies: Intelligence, Open Government and the Hutton Inquiry* (London: Social Affairs Unit, 2004), pp. 27–32.
11 This remains a sore point, especially with the Foreign Affairs Committee, which has consistently claimed that either it should oversee SIS and GCHQ or that the ISC should be replaced with a parliamentary select committee. See, for example, *The Decision to Go to War in Iraq*, HC 813-1 (London: TSO, 2003), pp. 5, 48–50.
12 The example of the complete failure of the public and media to note the public confessions in the media of the individuals who originally devised the prank of creating crop circles has been discussed at length by Carl Sagan in his *The Demon-Haunted World: Science as a Candle in the Dark* (New York: Headline, 1996).
13 See, for example, Monty Woodhouse, *Something Ventured* (London: Gollancz, 1983), p. 125.
14 For accounts of the US side of Boot/Ajax see, variously, Kermit Roosevelt, *Countercoup: The Struggle for the Control of Iran* (New York: McGraw-Hill, 1979), or, among the recent bubble of work on Iran based on released US documents, Stephen Kinzer, *All the Shah's Men: An American Coup and the Roots of Middle East Terror*

(Hoboken, NJ: John Wiley, 2003) and Mark J. Gasiorowski and Malcolm Burne (eds), *Mohammad Mossadeq and the 1953 Coup in Iran* (New York: Syracuse University Press, 2003).

15 Michael Herman, *Intelligence Power in Peace and War* (Cambridge: Cambridge University Press, 1996), pp. 294–304.

16 The papers concerning PBSUCCESS have been edited and published as part of the *Foreign Relations of the United States* series by the US Department of State (Washington, DC: US Government Printing Office, 2003), but the internal CIA history of the operation has also been published; see Nick Cullather, *Secret History: The CIA's Classified Account of its Operations in Guatemala 1952–1954* (Stanford, CA: Stanford University Press, 1999).

17 It should be recalled that it was Kennedy who made an issue of doing something about a communist Cuba during the 1960 televised election debate.

18 In retrospect, the prior experience relevant to the Bay of Pigs operation was not the coups in Iran or Guatemala, but the roundly unsuccessful efforts to organize armed resistance against Enver Hoxha's communist regime in Albania in the late 1940s. In many respects, the authoritative discussion of Zapata is the now-published CIA inspector general's report into the operation, and Deputy Director of Plans Richard Bissell's response to the report, edited by Peter Kornbluth as *Bay of Pigs Declassified: The Secret CIA Report on the Invasion of Cuba* (New York: The New Press, 1998).

19 Private information.

20 SIS mandate under the 1994 Intelligence Services Act is to operate 'outside the British islands', legislatively reinforcing the confinement of jurisdiction assigned to it under the 1931 Secret Service Committee confining it to actions outside the three-mile limit. *However*, it has retained jurisdiction over operations against targets *within* the three-mile limit that are legally foreign territory, such as embassies and trade delegations – since 1966 discharging this responsibility in collaboration with the Security Service via a cluster of joint sections.
See Philip H. J. Davies, *MI6 and the Machinery of Spying* (London: Frank Cass, 2004) pp. 275–78.

21 For a first-hand description of the role and authority of the FOA by a former incumbent, see Geoffrey McDermott, *The New Diplomacy and Its Apparatus* (London: Plume, 1973) p. 141. Detailed accounts of the Crabb disaster can be found on page 129 and in Davies, *MI6 and the Machinery of Spying*, pp. 229–33.

22 The Crabb affair was, in fact, more tragedy than conspiracy. The operation was not unprecedented: Crabb appears to have made a successful earlier dive under the *Sverdlov*, and, in fact, a second diver went underneath the *Ordzhonikidze* to successfully acquire the photographs Crabb was originally sent to get. In all likelihood, the ageing Crabb suffered a fatal heart attack during the long swim back around the headland to Gosport, where he had been put in the

water – indeed, he may already have been in distress at the time he was discovered by the crew of the cruiser.

23 See, for example, Tony Bunyan, *The History and Practice of the Political Police in Britain* (London: Quartet, 1978); J. Bloch and P. Fitzgerald, *British Intelligence and Covert Action* (London: Junction, 1983); Stephen Dorril, *The Silent Conspiracy* (London: Mandarin, 1994), as well as assorted pieces in his and Robin Ramsay's 'parapolitical' periodical *Lobster*, and various articles in the *New Statesman and Society* by Duncan Campbell, such as 'Friends and Others', 26 November 1982.

24 Peter Wright, *Spycatcher: The Candid Autobiography of a Senior Intelligence Officer* (Toronto: Stoddart, 1987), pp. 45–46.

25 *Report of the Committee of Privy Councillors Appointed to Enquire Into the Interception of Communications* (London: HMSO, 1957, Cmnd 283).

26 Some five years before IOCA, the Birkett Report was followed up with *The Interception of Communications in Great Britain* (London: HMSO, 1980, Cmnd 7873), which again specified the terms for approving a warrant, and gave warrant figures for the period 1958–79.

27 Michael Smith, *New Cloak, Old Dagger: How Britain's Spies Came in from the Cold* (London: Gollancz, 1996), pp. 66–67.

28 Anyone doubting Soviet success in penetrating the peace movement would be well advised to read Paul Mercer, *'Peace' of the Dead: The Truth Behind the Nuclear Disarmers* (London: Policy Research Publications, 1986); also Roy Godson and Richard Schulz, *Dezinformatsia: The Strategy of Soviet Disinformation* (New York: Berkeley, 1986).

29 Angus Mackenzie, *Secrets* (Berkeley, CA: University of California Press, 1997). A peculiarity of Mackenzie's account is his persistent efforts to try and find a rhetorical basis for condemnation of the CIA, even after the relatively anodyne nature of its activities become apparent from the actual evidence.

30 See L. Britt Snyder, 'Unlucky SHAMROCK: Recollections from the Church Committee's Investigation of NSA', *Studies in Intelligence*, winter 1999–2000, Unclassified Edition, pp. 43–52; and James G. Hudec, 'Unlucky SHAMROCK: The View from the Other Side', *Studies in Intelligence*, winter–spring 2001, Unclassified Edition No. 10, pp. 85–94.

31 William J. Dougherty, *Executive Secrets: Covert Action and the Presidency* (Lexington: University of Kentucky Press, 2004), p. 3.

32 Private information.

33 John Sawatsky, *Men in the Shadows: The Shocking Truth about the RCMP Security Service* (Toronto: Totem, 1980), *passim*.

34 It is impossible not to note that, given the recent failed prosecution of additional suspects in one of the most costly terrorist attacks ever in lives lost, Canadian finesse in this particular matter has evidently not improved.

35 Richard Cleroux, *Official Secret: The Inside Story of the Canadian Security Intelligence Service* (Toronto: McClelland and Stewart, 1991), p. 187.

36 It may be quite plausibly argued that, where one has surveillance without executive powers, as in the intelligence community, the activity is inherently less threatening to civil liberties in terms of the actual quality of life (rather than any fanciful and pseudo-religious notion of inherent 'human rights') in utilitarian terms if it has no palpable or observable impact on the conduct of activities and lives. The issue with surveillance should always be what is *done* with the resulting information, not whether it exists at all.

37 There have been some limited efforts in this direction, for example by one of the current authors. Philip Davies, in his *MI6 and the Machinery of Spying*, applies a range of microeconomic models to the British Secret Intelligence Service, including theories of the firm, Niskanen's bilateral monopoly theory of public service, and Garrett Hardin's 'tragedy of the commons'; see Ch. 7 therein *passim*.

38 For a detailed analysis of the bottom-line cost of the validation opportunity costs of collection during the financial stringency of the 1990s, see Philip H. J. Davies, 'Collection and Analysis on Iraq: Britain's Spy Machinery Breaks Down', *Studies in Intelligence* 49.4, December 2005.

39 Max Weber, *Economy and Society*, Vol. II (translated by Gunther Ross and Klaus Wittich) (London: Unwin University Books), p. 987.

40 Richard Rose, *Understanding Big Government* (London: Sage, 1984), pp. 166–67.

41 Andrew Dunsire, 'Testing Theories: the Contribution of Bureaumetrics', in Jan-Erik Lane, *Bureaucracy and Public Choice* (London: Sage, 1987).

42 F. H. Hinsley, E. E. Thomas, C. F. G. Ransom and R. C. Knight, *British Intelligence in the Second World War: Its Influence on Strategy and Operations*, Volume I (London: HMSO, 1979), p. 51.

43 See Nigel West, *The Secret War for the Falklands: The SAS, MI6 and the War Whitehall Nearly Lost* (London: Warner, 1998), p. 38; Mark Urban, *UK Eyes Alpha* (London: Faber, 1996), p. 10; and Lawrence Freedman, 'Intelligence Operations in the Falklands', *Intelligence and National Security*, Vol. 1, No. 3 (September 1986), *passim*.

44 Confidential conversation with senior UK official.

45 Lord Butler of Brockwell, *Review of Intelligence on Weapons of Mass Destruction* (London: TSO, 2004), p. 103.

46 Whether overproduction or excess demand dominates the US internal market for intelligence is an interesting question. In certain sectors, such as satellite development and production by the National Reconnaissance Office, the Niskanen hypothesis fits quite neatly (see, for example, William Odom, *Fixing Intelligence for a Secure America* (London: Yale University Press, 2003), pp. 73–76), as, arguably, does

the proliferation of analytical 'intelligence division'. On the other hand, signals and human intelligence seem to be more 'pull' driven.

47 Few reforms were more vigorously resisted in the US defence community than Robert Macnamara's imposition of line-item budgeting on the Department of Defense – before this the DoD had been all but a black hole for public money, and it still remains one of the US departments with the least (and the least effective) financial constraint.

48 This is perhaps the only point on which both Robert Steele and Loch K. Johnson agree in their debate conducted in the pages of *Journal of Conflict Studies* ('Virtual Intelligence: Conflict Avoidance and Resolution through Information Peacekeeping', *Journal of Conflict Studies* 29, pp. 69–105) and *Foreign Policy* ('Spies', in *Foreign Policy* 120, pp. 18–24), respectively.

49 See, for example, United States Congress, *Joint Inquiry into Intelligence Activities Before and After the Terrorist Attacks of September 11, 2001: Report of the Senate Select Committee on Intelligence and the House Permanent Select Committee on Intelligence Together with Additional Views* (Washington, DC: United States Congress, 2002) and Senate Select Committee on Intelligence, *Report on the US Intelligence Community's Prewar Assessments on Iraq* (Washington, DC: United States Congress, 2004).

50 Fulvio Martini, 'Discussion', in Harold Shukman (ed.), *Agents for Change* (London: St Ermins, 2000), pp. 72–73.

51 Sub-Committee on Defence Policy and Requirements, 'Defence Requirements Enquiry: Re SIS Funds in Defence Requirements: Programmes of the Defence Services (Paper)', 3/36, Enclosure 1 in CAB 16/123, The National Archive.

52 For a detailed account and robust advocacy of the virtues of line-item budgeting in intelligence, see Odom, *Fixing Intelligence for a More Secure America*, pp. 32, 73.

53 Confidential conversation with former senior US intelligence official.

54 Only in autumn of 2003 did the US system shift to a comparable requirements cycle, administered by the director of central intelligence on a six-monthly basis, as articulated in National Security Presidential Directive (NSPD) 26. Private information.

55 Cabinet Office, *National Intelligence Machinery* (London: TSO, 2001), pp. 9, 17 and private information. It should be noted that MI5's domestic investigation brief is only partly bounded by the NIRP, as it is supposed to stand independent of party political interest, and to focus its attention purely on threats to the 'realm' and parliamentary democracy as such.

56 Herman, *Intelligence Power in Peace and War*, p. 292.

57 Interview with senior UK intelligence official.

58 Interviews with two senior UK government officials.

59 As specified under the 1974 Hughes–Ryan Amendment to the 1961 Foreign Assistance Act.

60 Risk aversion in the CIA was a major issue in the first Reagan administration, when William Casey, once a clandestine operator in the wartime Office of Strategic Services, took over as DCI. See, for example, Bob Woodward, *Veil: The Secret Wars of the CIA, 1981–1987* (New York: Simon & Schuster, 1987), pp. 4–9.

61 See, variously, *Report of the Joint Congressional Committee into the Terrorist Attacks of September 11, 2001*, pp. 279–303; *Report of the 9/11 Commission* (Washington, DC: US Government Printing Office, 2004), pp. 126–33; Michael Scheuer (writing as 'Anonymous'), *Imperial Hubris: Why the West is Losing the War on Terror* (Washington, DC: Brassey's, 2004); James Bamford, *A Pretext for War: 9/11, Iraq and the Abuse of America's Intelligence Agencies* (New York: Doubleday, 2004); and, most recently, Robert Baer, 'Spies Unlike Us', *Foreign Policy*, March/April 2005.

62 For a detailed account of the CIA's encounters with Iran-Contra, see, for example, Bob Woodward, *Veil*.

63 Stephen Lander, 'The Oversight of Security and Intelligence', presented to the Security and Intelligence Studies Group and Royal United Services Institute joint conference on a five-year review of the ISC's activity in 2001, p. 5.

64 Quoted, for example, in a Tom King lecture given at the Security and Intelligence Studies Group and Royal United Services Institute joint conference on a five-year review of the ISC's activity in 2001.

65 Glees and Davies, *Spinning the Spies*, pp. 18–20; this argument is derived from a prior formulation in 1987 by Ken Robertson, 'The Politics of Secret Intelligence', in Robertson (ed.), *British and American Approaches to Intelligence* (London: Macmillan, 1987), *passim*.

66 The term is chosen with reference to just such an evasion of ministerial responsibility in the wake of the 1966 Aberfan disaster, when 144 people were killed by a coal-waste tip that slid onto the village of that name.

67 Private information. James Adams, *The New Spies: Exploring the Frontiers of Espionage* (London: Hutchinson, 1994), pp. 101–02.

68 Currently the Interception of Communications Commissioner (Sir Swinton Thomas) and the Intelligence Services Commissioner (Lord Brown of Eaton-under-Heywood).

69 K. G. Robertson, 'Accountable Intelligence: the British Experience'; Geoffrey R. Weller, 'The Canadian Security Intelligence Service under Stress', *Canadian Journal of Public Administration*, Vol. 31, No. 2 (summer, 1988), pp. 279–302.

70 The ISC would no doubt argue that, in its 1999–2000 annual report (pp. 22–25), it flagged up GCHQ's massive underestimate of the transition costs involved in moving to its new HQ before the monies were committed. But, as noted, in fact they only registered GCHQ's own revised figures, which GCHQ was not attempting to hide.

71 William Niskanen, *Bureaucracy: Servant or Master? Lessons from America* (London: Institute of Economic Affairs, 1973).
72 Herman, *Intelligence Power in Peace and War*, pp. 291–96.
73 K. G. Robertson, 'Recent Reform of Intelligence in the UK: Democratization or Risk Management?', *Intelligence and National Security* 13:2 (summer 1998), p. 154. It might plausibly be argued that this is something of a reversal of Robertson's 1987 view, set out in *British and American Approaches to Intelligence*.
74 As articulated, of course, in their seminal television series and books, *Yes, Minister* and *Yes, Prime Minister*.
75 Hugh Trevor-Roper's description of the interwar SIS; see *The Philby Affair* (London: William Kimber, 1968), p. 69.
76 Roy Hattersley's complaint about the Security Service during the debate on the 1989 Security Service Act in *Hansard*, vol. 145, 16 January 1989, Cols 36–42. Given the tone of the Security Commission concerning MI5 management during its inquiry into Michael Bettaney's attempted treachery, Hattersley's complaints may not have been entirely unsound; *Report of the Security Commission* (London: HMSO, 1985, Cmnd 9514).
77 The regular meetings of the ISC can be contrasted with the infrequent convocations of the Security Commission, which never meets unless it is needed to investigate a security scandal, and then usually with a new membership.
78 At the time of the joint inquiry into 9/11, the House was Republican dominated and the HPSCI chair was Porter Goss (now DCI), and the Senate was Democrat led with Bob Graham as SSCI chair.
79 A detailed account of a lengthy series of such suits can be found in Mackenzie's *Secrets*.
80 See, for example, Gill, *Policing Politics*, pp. 293–96.
81 This constitutional notion is hardly unique to the British situation, nor contingent upon an American doctrine of the Separation of Powers. This is precisely the view held by members of parliamentary committees in the Canadian government. Confidential conversation with a member of the Canadian Interim Committee on Security and Intelligence.
82 One could draw a comparison with the repeated call in the UK for 'more Bobbies on the beat' – a presence that the police know is a waste of manpower, but that increases public confidence.
83 The total failure of the UK government's inquiry into the complete absence of any real health implications from cell phone radio masts, for wholly and hollowly political reasons, is a classic example. For a telling critique of this kind of problem, see Christie Davies and Mark Neil, *The Corporation Under Siege* (London: Social Affairs Unit, 1998).

CHAPTER 4

THE ISC IN ACTION – 10 YEARS OF OVERSIGHT UK-STYLE

A JOB WELL DONE?

Before considering the effectiveness of the ISC, we must enter an important caveat: the ISC cannot be held responsible for any government's refusal to accept its recommendations. It has discharged its statutory responsibilities when it delivers its reports to the prime minister and subsequently Parliament. Whatever its findings, the government always has the option, in theory at least, of rejecting or effectively ignoring them (though it now accepts that it must at least do the Committee the courtesy of responding to each of its findings).

In 2002, for example, the ISC slated the Security Service over its inability to provide the correct threat assessment for British visitors going to Indonesia, where, on 12 October 2002, over 190 people were murdered in a terrorist attack. While the ISC concluded that 'no action could have been taken to prevent the attacks', it added crisply that the Security Service 'had not assessed the threat correctly and therefore did not raise the level of threat' (it had been set at 'significant' level three for diplomats, and 'significant' level four for other Britons, despite evidence of considerable Al Qaeda activity).[1]

However, the government made it very clear, in its reply to the ISC, that it did *not* accept that the Security Service had erred and, although it noted the ISC's recommendation that the threat-level calibration system be altered, it said that the Security Service was doing this in any case, *despite* the ISC's comments.[2] The significance of the government response became apparent in July 2005, when it emerged that, in the weeks prior to the attacks, the Security Service once again got the threat level wrong, lowering it rather than raising it.

Yet it is one thing to make a recommendation and to be rebuffed; quite another to miss the need for a recommendation in the first place. It is, therefore, vital to examine the work of the ISC in order to ascertain whether, in general, and over the most important issues, it was correctly identifying the problem areas and was making the necessary recommendations for change, reform and improvement.

Our queries may seem to involve simplistic formulations about matters that are, in reality, deeply complex fields of specialist professional activity. Yet they express the doubts that Parliament, media and the public will raise, and to provide answers to them is vital. Rightly or wrongly, intelligence and security matters are seen to impact more deeply on our nation's life, and on its security and well-being, than almost any other. They affect the very nature of our government, the policies that it pursues, and the balance between security and individual liberties. They inevitably prompt reflection on the way in which Britain uses intelligence to shape its national policies, and whether the ISC has done enough to ensure that, where this happens, it is done in the best possible way.

Whether broad or narrow, all our questions really boil down to one: how can the ISC help sustain our security and restore public *trust* both in the intelligence services and in the government's management of them? That the ISC has a vital role to play in Britain's future security cannot be doubted. Does its past performance suggest it will do this as well as it needs to?

We address these issues below, drawing, in particular, on unique and generously given interviews, for the public record, by the first two chairs of the ISC, Lord (Tom) King of Bridgwater and Lady (Ann) Taylor of Bolton, and also with Sir David Omand, Security and Intelligence Co-ordinator to the Cabinet from 2002 until 2005, and one of Britain's most experienced intelligence experts (whose first formal on-the-record interview since his retirement was given for the purposes of this study). We also benefited from discussions with other former senior 'insiders' who spoke to us on condition of confidentiality.

These interviews illuminate not only the way in which the work of the ISC impacts on our national political life, but also on the way in which it has come to regard itself, and was, and is, regarded within Whitehall and Westminster. They shed light on those areas of politics that the written record alone cannot fully explain: the political independence of the ISC (given its particular and peculiar status as a creation of the prime minister); the ISC's view of the mechanisms by which Tony Blair received secret intelligence, and the quality of the advice about it that he was given. They also shed light on the provenance of the September Dossier, and the major success scored by the JIC in preventing Alastair Campbell from writing it. The quality of ISC reports is examined, as is the power possessed by the heads of the secret Agencies to keep the deepest secrets of their services. Our interviewees provided new insights into the nature of the intelligence failures that have dogged Britain since 9/11, as well as the potential remedies and the prospects for a brighter future for the entire British intelligence community.

On the credit side, it can be shown that the ISC has managed, without additional legislation, continually to extend its investigative brief into new and previously hidden areas of intelligence activity. This is no mean achievement, and the ISC's first two chairs, Tom King and Ann Taylor, are rightly very proud of it. But, as we noted in Chapter 2, there are statutory limits on what the ISC is entitled to see. Even though the agency heads may choose to take the Committee into their confidence, there will always be 'no-go' areas that the ISC will not be allowed to penetrate. As David Omand put it to us:

> The intelligence Agencies are different from other parts of government – they work in secrecy and 'the need to know'. They have sensitive overseas liaisons. If they don't have confidence their material will be safeguarded, they won't want to tell you and you are unlikely to find out by external examination.

In the event, the ISC has clearly managed to gain the trust of the UK Agencies – not an end in itself, of course (and, as we explain, itself something of a minefield), but a real success none the less. The ISC has probed numerous complex and technologically challenging areas, and undertaken a continuing programme of overseas visits to compare notes with analogous oversight bodies in an attempt to establish best practice. The ISC reports are always exceptionally interesting; despite the redactions required on security grounds they often make information public for the first time. They are a vital resource for all students of the British intelligence community, although they receive far too little attention. All of these things (and this list is not exhaustive) are major and significant achievements. They should not be belittled, and it is not the purpose of this book to do so.

On the debit side, however, there are three main charges that can be made against the ISC. They can be summarized as follows:

- First, that the Committee stumbled badly over the all-important issue of the non-existent Iraqi weapons of mass destruction (WMD), whose long shadow will dominate British domestic politics and the UK's foreign policy-making for many years to come. The charge here is not that the ISC failed at the time to spot the inadequacies of Britain's secret intelligence on WMD and that the Humint was almost certainly being oversold by the SIS – that would have been asking too much. Rather, it is that its inquiry after the event was too tightly focused, and that it should have investigated, as the Butler Committee later did, all aspects of the WMD fiasco. This would have required it to obtain the same powers as Butler (e.g. to obtain information on intelligence sources), but the precedent of the Mitrokhin inquiry showed that the ISC could demand greater powers of access if this was necessary to carry out its tasks. Instead it can be accused of having taken an over-narrow view of its responsibilities in establishing what went wrong.

- The second charge is that the ISC has failed to generate *public* and arguably *parliamentary* trust in the secret Agencies of the British government – the ISC's core function. As Tom King put it to us:

> The ISC has a real role to play in establishing trust between the Agencies *and the public*. [our emphasis]

He added:

> When the ISC began its work in 1995, it had been important for the Agencies to come in 'from behind the curtain' and engage more with the public. They quickly saw the point.

But that trust may be seen to have been eroded since 2001. It appears that Michael Howard (then leader of the Conservative Party) and Charles Kennedy (then leader of the Liberal Democrats) did not believe the ISC was sufficiently impartial to conduct what was to become the Butler review. This is a grave indictment, and we look at it in more detail below. But we can point also to the public and parliamentary scepticism which met the intelligence on WMD (deflected from its rightful target, SIS, onto the prime minister and the government, which believed it) or to the failure of Parliament to support the 90-day detention period proposed by the prime minister in the government's counter-terrorism bill, despite his insistence that it was a measure which the security services desired. Nor can one ignore the difficulties repeatedly experienced in the courts, where the lack of success in gaining convictions in cases where the security services believe there is strong intelligence-based evidence suggests the intelligence assessments are often not accepted.[3]

- The third and final charge is that, in its many reports, the ISC has generally granted the intelligence community a cleaner bill of health than the facts warranted, appearing more ready to give out compliments than criticism, and arguably too willing to accept the Agencies' own estimations of their worth. An example of this is its handling of the terrorist threat to the UK. In its 2004–05 report, the Committee recognized that

> [t]he threat from international terrorism, essentially from Islamic extremist groups, is ever present and global in its nature and reach.[4]

However, the Committee gave the impression that the threat was essentially external to the UK, and had to do with individuals and not networks. It also failed to reinforce the message others – not least Sir John Stevens, the then Metropolitan Police commissioner – were conveying: that a terrorist attack on London was inevitable; not 'if' but 'when'. In March 2004 Stevens had warned:

> It would be miraculous if, with all the terrorist resources arranged against us, terrorists did not get through, and given that some are prepared to give their own lives, it would be inconceivable that someone does not get through to London.[5]

The net outcome of this is that public opinion has been encouraged to believe that the oversight provided by the ISC meant that things were, generally, 'A-OK', when, in fact, a more neutral line on the things that were going well, and stronger statements about the things that were not satisfactory, might have generated greater public awareness of the security dangers.

These charges, stated so baldly, may seem to some to be unduly severe and sweeping, but we would suggest there is evidence to sustain some of them in part, if not always in whole. They are certainly issues that should be addressed, not least by the ISC itself. There is, it should be added at once, also evidence from within the ISC and the intelligence community to suggest that its sins (both of commission and omission) should not be exaggerated; we have attempted to provide a balanced assessment.

THE COMMITTEE'S REPORTS TO THE PRIME MINISTER AND THE NATION

Before attempting to draw up an audit of the auditor – the ISC – we should begin our analysis by examining the Committee's own published reports. We are very conscious that we have not attempted to cover every subject addressed by the Committee during its decade-plus of life; there is much to be covered by future researchers.[6] Rather, we have selected those issues that, we consider, cast most light on the ISC's various relationships with the Agencies, the wider UK intelligence community, the prime minister and his ministerial colleagues, Parliament, the media, and the public.

Rather than ploughing through the Committee's published products in chronological order, we have chosen to start with the ISC's most recent annual report[7] and the themes it touches on, many of which flow from earlier investigations of the same concerns. We then examine some other issues running through the years.

If our assertions about the importance of the issue of Iraqi WMD are accepted, then this report must indeed be the first to be discussed, because it was, for the ISC, a real opportunity to square up to how the condition of British intelligence (particularly the SIS) had developed by spring 2005 when the report was written. It was, by then, clear to everyone that SIS had failed to provide key accurate WMD intelligence. It was also obvious that Britain's intelligence assessment mechanisms had failed to ensure that the judgements on which the prime minister and his government had to rely in making critical policy decisions were accurate. These are issues of major political and constitutional importance. Yet the ISC's handling of these matters fell considerably short of what the public had a right to expect.

The British public (and not only the British public) continues, rightly or wrongly, to regard the existence of secret intelligence on Iraqi WMD as being the overriding reason why Britain and the United States of America attacked Iraq. This was the inescapable conclusion of the arguments contained implicitly in the September 2002 WMD dossier and explicitly in President Bush's State of the Union speech of 29 January 2003:

> The world has waited 12 years for Iraq to disarm. America will not accept a serious and mounting threat to our country, and our friends and our allies. The United States will ask the U.N. Security Council to convene on February the 5th to consider the facts of Iraq's ongoing defiance of the world. Secretary of State Powell will present information and intelligence about Iraqi's – Iraq's illegal weapons programs, its attempts to hide those weapons from inspectors, and its links to terrorist groups.

The British prime minister and the US president had clearly decided to make the supposed existence of Iraqi WMD the *casus belli* justifying invasion. As President Bush put it in the same speech:

> We will consult. But let there be no misunderstanding: If Saddam Hussein does not fully disarm, for the safety of our people and for the peace of the world, we will lead a coalition to disarm him.

David Omand played down the significance of intelligence as the real driver of war:

> We did not go to war because of specific pieces of faulty WMD intelligence, although we all accept that there were some of those.

We now know that he is perfectly right when he speaks of the motor driving the prime minister's high policy. But it was the government's choice to make the supposed threat from Iraqi WMD the cornerstone of its public case for armed intervention. For that reason, WMD intelligence, if not the sole trigger for war, was, beyond a shadow of a doubt in the public's mind, the major reason why Iraq had to be invaded at that particular time. It is hard to disagree with Tom King's comment that 'the government is still in denial over Iraq' (he believes the ISC should not let the issue go). He suggests that 'when historians come to write about the WMD issue, an important question will be: "how did the government get away with it?"'

We should recall that, in explaining (in January 2006) why the evidence he presented to the United Nations on 5 February 2003 on

Iraqi WMD was so badly wrong, former US Secretary of State Colin Powell said it was because

> ...the intelligence community got it wrong...I thought it was a fact because intelligence said so. We were wrong. The intelligence community was wrong. The British intelligence community was wrong. Everyone believed it was true at the time...There were no stockpiles. The error was that we believed he had matched his intentions to his capabilities. That was wrong, it was proven to be wrong. I was wrong because I had the wrong information...[8]

Powell did not dissent from the view that this whole matter had been a 'fiasco'.

On 11 April 2005 the ISC published its 2004–05 report, at a time when it was already perfectly clear from Lord Butler's review that the WMD question was indeed a very major one.[9] The ISC's report was, in fact, completed 'early', prior to the general election of 5 May 2005 (and, we suggest, lacked substantive weight as a result, though Ann Taylor denies this), in order to allow publication prior to the dissolution of Parliament (and hence the ISC).

The report appeared when media attention was focused on the forthcoming election and scant attention was paid to its findings. This was regrettable, not just because some of them were intrinsically of great interest, but also because of the things that the report left out, or treated with less firmness and clarity than they merited. Was it the case that the ISC believed it did not wish to unduly embarrass a government seeking re-election? If this were proved to be true, it would, of course, undermine the entire concept of impartial oversight. But *is* it true? We will go on to consider how far the ISC may or may not be swayed by political considerations.

It is certainly a fact that the ISC had the opportunity in this report to be every bit as forthright as Colin Powell. What is more, it needed to be so, in order to do something to protect its own reputation, given its previous inability to get to the bottom of the issue, as outlined below. The 2004–05 report does, indeed, contain some criticisms of the government and the Agencies. However, the very preface to the report makes it clear that its main thrust is likely to be guarded, and that no attempt will be made to draw blood either from its own back or from the backs of others. The preface states that

[w]hilst this Report contains a number of criticisms and concerns…we would not wish these points to overshadow the essential and *excellent* work that the Agencies have undertaken. As ever, much of this work will never be reported and therefore we wish to place on record our appreciation of the staff within the UK Intelligence Community. Without their work, *the UK would not have been protected against terrorist attack.*[10] [our emphases]

Yet within three months of the publication of this report, it became chillingly clear that the UK was *not* being protected against terrorist attacks. On the issue of WMD, the ISC in its final annual report had a real opportunity to correct its own earlier findings (and failings) contained in its special report on Iraqi WMD, dated September 2003.[11] As we shall see, it was important that this major intelligence shortcoming was addressed properly – both for the national purpose and for the reputation of the ISC itself, which had not got to the root of the problem (particularly since Lord Butler had done so, speaking softly yet wielding a big stick).

But the ISC really does seem to have failed to deliver. In paragraph 60 of its report, in reviewing the findings of the Butler inquiry and the way in which the government was seeking to draw lessons from Lord Butler's recommendations, the ISC noted meekly that, on 20 July 2004, the government had confirmed that the SIS had 'formally withdrawn the line of Iraqi WMD-related intelligence, which had been reported by the Butler Review as having been withdrawn, in July 2003'. Coyly, it explained that 'this line of reporting had been important in the crafting of the September 2002 dossier' and that 'the Prime Minister, the Foreign Secretary and a small number of officials had been *orally* briefed on it by the SIS but it had been withheld from WMD experts in the DIS' (our emphasis). The ISC concluded: 'We do not believe that this was the appropriate way of handling the material.' To term this process 'not…appropriate' is an overwhelmingly bland way of indicating not just that the chief of SIS (Sir Richard Dearlove) had been permitted by Tony Blair, Jack Straw and a few officials to advise him in this way, but that the intelligence so provided proved to be wholly incorrect.

To add an element of insult to this episode, the ISC noted, *en passant,* that it was only in July 2004 that the prime minister had been informed that the intelligence was wrong, when the Butler review made this public (a fact spotted first by John Ware of BBC's

Panorama). In what was, perhaps, its understatement of 2005, the ISC conceded that it was now '…concerned at the amount of intelligence on Iraqi WMD that has now had to be withdrawn by the SIS'.[12] It was also worried about the fact that the SIS had failed to tell either the prime minister or the foreign secretary about its intelligence doubts immediately it became aware of them. SIS's failure to inform the prime minister and foreign secretary that an absolutely key input into their foreign policy-making was, in fact, entirely unreliable was, to be quite blunt, nothing short of disgraceful. It would be deemed scarcely credible had it not been verified by both Butler and the ISC.

In fact, paragraphs 60–63 of the ISC's 2004–05 annual report are so understated that it is hard to see how they could have any political impact either during the election or internally, in improving the procedures and systems within the British intelligence community. We need only recall what Lord Butler did with the same material. We would suggest that Ann Taylor's view – that because Butler had done it the ISC no longer needed to – rather misses the point: the ISC should have done it first because it is a statutory body in continuous session, charged with overseeing the secret Agencies. Lord Butler's review was a one-off. In addition, the ISC should have added its own conclusions and suggestions, not least because it had been as seriously misled by SIS as the prime minister himself.

The outgoing ISC was equally feeble when considering the JIC's assessments of Iraq's WMD programmes and capabilities. The JIC had itself conducted a thorough review of the intelligence on Iraqi WMD (which Lord Butler had said was 'open to doubt and seriously flawed') and had come to the conclusion that, although its assessments had been right to suggest that Saddam had possessed nuclear ambitions, he had actually possessed *no* nuclear capability. Contrary to the JIC's 2002 assessment on ballistic missiles, it was now clear that Iraq had *not* possessed the 20 Al-Hussein missiles the JIC had previously assumed to exist (although there was some evidence that its scientists were working on the development of medium-range missiles). Finally, the ISC stated that, in 2002, the JIC had judged that Iraq might retain stocks of chemical agents, could produce significant quantities of mustard gas within weeks, and significant quantities of Sarin and VX within months. Yet in 2004 it became obvious that, despite a 'possible intention' to do so, this judgement had also 'not been substantiated'.[13]

The ISC's failure to confront, in any focused way, the implications of all of this in its 2004–05 report is a curious omission: it had been briefed on substantive intelligence assessments prior to the invasion (for which the Committee duly expressed its gratitude) and had subsequently produced, in September 2003, its own report *Iraqi Weapons of Mass Destruction – Intelligence and Assessments*.[14] But that report only sought '...to examine whether the available intelligence, which informed the decision to invade Iraq, was adequate and properly assessed and whether it was accurately reflected in Government publications'. As Tom King wryly noted,

> [i]t took Hutton and Butler to demand sight of HMG's emails – the ISC had not thought of this; my own experience was always – if you don't ask for it, you won't get it.

What is more, in its 2002–03 annual report, the ISC had publicly declared (in paragraph 80) that 'the Committee is grateful to the JIC Chairman and "C" for the regular briefings by which we have been kept up to date before and during the military action against Iraq, *as it was intelligence that indicated the Iraqis were continuing to produce WMD and their delivery means*...' (our emphasis).

In its report on Iraqi WMD, the ISC stated that it had been examining the matter since 1998. The purpose of this report, however, was '...to examine whether the available intelligence *which informed the decision to invade Iraq* was adequately and properly assessed and whether it was accurately reflected in Government publications' (our emphasis). It added, quite sensibly considering its formal responsibilities, 'this Report does not judge whether the decision to invade Iraq was correct'.

Tony Blair, the ISC said, had permitted it to go through all the JIC assessments and interview, as he said, 'those people in the security services [sic] who drew up the JIC reports'. That, said Blair, '"is surely a fair way to proceed. I will then publish the report."'[15] On 16 July 2003, Parliament voted for a motion proposing that the ISC was 'the appropriate body to consider the intelligence relating to Iraq'. But the resulting report, produced less than eight weeks later, was far from the exposé some may have expected.

To be fair, the ISC did cover some of the ground later tilled more effectively by Butler; for example, in considering the value of Humint it described how 'sources' could include the information provided by 'sub-sources' or even 'sub-sub-sources' but went on (in paragraph 26) to affirm its confidence in 'single source reporting':

Some of the intelligence that agents produce cannot be verified or corroborated by intelligence from other sources. The professional judgement of the agent's reliability is based on all that is known about the agent and their circumstances... It is possible to recruit a reliable agent with exceptional access to high-grade intelligence. Examples of agents with unique access are Oleg Gordievsky, Vasili Mitrokhin from the Cold War and Vladimir Pasechnik who reported on Russian biological war programmes. These are amongst the most valuable agents the UK has ever had. Each was the origin of 'single source' reporting from the SIS. For much of that reporting there was no collateral intelligence from other sources.

No one would deny the value of single-source reporting, provided the source is sound; it appears the ISC believed it was safe to rely on the intelligence that SIS was providing because, crudely put, it was a given that SIS was very good at its job. Not just the ISC; one of the authors of this book (John Morrison) said on *Panorama*.

> I think you've got to realize that the staff at MI6 are professionals. It's not in their interest just to believe what they're told. If they say they've got a good source, then they have got a good source. What they can't say is they guarantee that everything that source says is correct.[16]

It is the only thing in the interview he now regrets having said – but at the time most, if not all, in the UK intelligence community would have been equally confident of SIS's professionalism in assessing the worth of their sources.

Yet in 2004, just one year after publishing its 2003 report on Iraqi WMD, the ISC could be found pointing out that, in July 2003, SIS had withdrawn its line of reporting about WMD. This means that, just when the ISC was busy accepting SIS's validation of its own collection systems, SIS was itself, internally, discounting them. At the very time the ISC was considering 'whether the available intelligence which informed the decision to invade Iraq was adequately and properly assessed', SIS had concluded the intelligence was wholly flawed. Why did the ISC not subsequently make more of a fuss about this? Did the ISC suffer from 'groupthink' of its own? Was it bamboozled by the aura surrounding SIS? These are matters to which we must return.

In September 2003, at any rate, the ISC affirmed (quite correctly) in paragraph 32 of its report that

> Iraq was a hard target but the SIS ran a number of agents against Iraq and Saddam's regime. These agents produced intelligence over a wide range of topics although the SIS acknowledged that coverage on some subjects was stronger than on others.

Despite the ISC's understanding that there were some things the JIC knew that it did not know (for example, the location or readiness of missile sites), it said categorically (in paragraph 66):

> ...based on the intelligence and the JIC assessments we have seen, we accept that there was convincing evidence that Iraq had active chemical, biological and nuclear programmes and the capability to produce chemical and biological weapons. Iraq was continuing to develop ballistic missiles. All these activities were prohibited...

It is perfectly true that the ISC did 'have a go' at the MoD. Alluding to the 'Kelly Affair' and the '45-minute warning', it stated:

> We regard the initial failure by the MoD to disclose that some staff had put their concerns in writing to their line managers as unhelpful and potentially misleading. This is not excused by the genuine belief within the DIS that the concerns had been expressed as part of the normal lively debate that often surrounds draft JIC Assessments within the DIS. We are disturbed that after the first evidence session, which did not cover all the concerns raised by the DIS staff, the Defence Secretary decided against giving instructions for a letter to be written to us outlining the concerns.[17]

It is clear from the Committee's reports over the years that one of the main things that irritated them was a department's or agency's failure to 'come clean' about a problem at an early stage.

We are not damning the ISC's 2004–05 annual report *in toto*; where it concentrated on essentially administrative matters it was fine, even if, as we maintain, it pulled its punches on substantive intelligence issues such as the failures of SIS and the JIC over Iraqi WMD. Reading the report, one gains the impression that the Committee had rather run out of steam when it came to significant intelligence concerns, concentrating on the machinery of the intelligence community rather than its *raison d'être*.

THE DOSSIER AND BEYOND

The dossier, in Lord Butler's view (and ours), ought never to have been published:

> …the publication of such a document in the name and with the authority of the JIC had the result that more weight was placed on the intelligence than it would bear. The consequence also was to put the JIC and its Chairman into an area of public controversy and arrangements must be made for the future which avoid putting the JIC and its Chairman in a similar position.[18]

That aside, and considering only its content, the main body of the document was not as bad as has often been suggested, and accurately reflected the then JIC assessments of Iraq's WMD programmes and capabilities. As David Omand interestingly attests, one key victory scored by the intelligence community was that it, rather than No. 10 and in particular Alastair Campbell, was tasked with writing it (though this revelation prompts the question: what made Campbell believe he ought to have written it?). As David Omand explained:

> The agency heads and the JIC were united in wanting the JIC chair to author it, since they wished to prevent information officers (or Alastair Campbell) from writing it. This was because the latter would not appreciate the nuances in JIC assessment. John Scarlett took a huge amount of flak about this. In fact, he stood up to Alastair Campbell, and probably took more public flak than was necessary. But Butler and his Committee realized this, and reflected it in their recommendation concerning John Scarlett's next job [as chief of SIS].

To be fair to the ISC, it had noted in its 2003 report that Scarlett had said on 5 September 2002 he would take responsibility for the dossier only if he were 'given complete control of the contents', and that this was subsequently agreed in writing by Alastair Campbell.[19] Reading between the lines, the nature of the battle that was going on here is not hard to discern, and nor is its outcome. But we have to read between the lines; it is not there in black and white. And there is nothing about the constitutional niceties of this fight. Why not?

David Omand was, in fact, much more forthright (in 2005) about the errors in the dossier than the ISC (in 2003). He said, for example:

> The 45-minute warning should never have appeared, but none of this was the deciding factor, it was a second-division issue. The Agencies were reluctant to provide any detail for the dossier because of source sensitivities, and when the 45-minute report appeared it was taken as 'colour' to help explain the issue, and avoid just assertion.

The ISC simply said the reference to 45 minutes 'lacked precision'.[20]

Omand went on to comment:

Butler was right to criticize the lack of questioning [by the committee drafting the dossier]. They could have produced a better report just before the final decisions. The Butler Report noted that the intelligence had been hardening up, but the question was whether that was a real effect of fresh new intelligence that threw genuine new light [on the subject], or whether it was because with war approaching and MoD in particular concerned over sending soldiers into a CBW environment, the search was intensified quickly for any relevant intelligence, and that was sweeping up material that was not of first quality. Butler asked: should there not have been another JIC assessment before final decisions were taken; should there not have been a reappraisal in the light of nil returns from the arms inspectors? This all had to do with the reality of war approaching.

As we have seen, the ISC also thought the publication of the dossier made sense (Ann Taylor today still insists that 'we should be mature enough to listen to what the Agencies are saying'). However, despite their agreement with each other on this point, the wider question is raised as to why the ISC did not produce the report that became the Butler review? David Omand says that Ann Taylor was 'cross' that it had been Butler and not the ISC who was given this particular task. She may be even more cross at his reasons for why the ISC was denied it. He outlined the fact that

> …the need to handle Parliament and the media meant giving it more credibility through having non-political as well as political figures. So we ended up with the chair of the ISC and

the deputy chair [sic] plus an ex-CDS [chief of defence staff] and an ex-PUS [permanent under secretary] plus Butler.

For her part, Ann Taylor noted the realities of the situation at the time:

> The way in which the ISC was dovetailing into the Butler Committee inquiry should not be ignored, not only because two of the five members of the Butler Committee were members of the ISC. The ISC did its report on the WMD and then the Butler Committee did its and commented on and followed up many aspects of the ISC report. Butler built on what the ISC had done. Butler also suggested ways in which the ISC could follow up aspects of that committee's recommendations. To do what Butler had done would have been to repeat his work.
>
> It is true that the ISC could have conducted a Butler-type inquiry and were willing to do so, but the other Parties did not agree to this. Charles Kennedy and Michael Howard made this clear for the Liberal Democrats and the Conservatives. No. 10 was indeed seriously considering letting the ISC do the report and I had said to the PM that I would be happy for the ISC to do it. Blair had also said in Parliament that he would have been content for the ISC. Even when Butler was proposed, it had originally been thought that three ISC members and three others might undertake the work, but Kennedy said no.

But when asked whether she regretted not having written the Butler review, she said (no doubt in full knowledge of how much effort eventually went into Butler):

> No, there would have been so much work for the members of the ISC and it would have been very difficult.

Did she think the ISC had lost some credibility because it had not written the review?

> No. Our reports on WMD and the Bali bombing were the most significant of all the reports we wrote. They developed new ground rules concerning access, and other rules.

But it was Butler, not the ISC, who went beyond the question 'was the intelligence assessed appropriately?' to ask 'was the intelligence right in the first place?' The ISC has never had access as of right to raw intelligence; had it conducted a Butler-type review it could have insisted on the same degree of openness from SIS about its sources, thus setting a precedent for future inquiries. And yet one feels that the ISC, with its minimal staff support and competing imperatives, would never have been able to produce so thorough and trenchant a report as did Lord Butler's team.

It is worth emphasizing that Sir Christopher Meyer, whose ambassadorial memoir shows he was not a personal fan of the Blair government (though always its loyal servant when serving as a diplomat), says unequivocally that the secret intelligence about WMD that he saw supported the line being taking by the prime minister. However, intriguingly, he concedes the possibility (which he does not explore) that the prime minister was being told what he wanted to hear:

> Enormous controversy surrounds the intelligence on which Blair and Bush relied. I myself saw a great deal of intelligence material in 2002. I was myself persuaded that Iraq had WMD. There is nothing of which I am aware which Blair said in public about the intelligence for which he did not have cover either from the JIC or from its Chairman, John Scarlett. If either succumbed to political pressure that is another story. Had I been in Campbell's place, I too would have wanted as categorical a public depiction of Saddam's threat as possible. Equally I would have expected the JIC to be rigorous in telling me how far to go.[21]

Like Sir Christopher Meyer, Ann Taylor told us that she could not be certain that Blair (who had long decided that he thought Saddam deserved to be removed) had always been given the full facts, and that he had not, on occasion, been told what, it might be assumed, he wished to hear. She said:

> You have to be willing to tell the prime minister what is what. Too many people pull punches with the prime minister. You should never tell ministers what they want to hear. It would do them a disservice. But it needs to be done in a proper way.

David Omand was perhaps more ready to see shortcomings in the ISC's failure to dissect the WMD issue, but argued the need to see the matter in perspective:

> The WMD issue as myth [sic] is now a major cross for the intelligence community and it will have to bear it for a very

long time. It would be unfortunate if UK intelligence was tainted because of it, which is why it was very helpful to have Lord Butler detail the major WMD successes in his report. Iraq WMD was not representative of agency performance.

He added:

There is no connection between this matter and the way that analysis of intelligence is conducted in the war on terror. Policy towards protective security has to be made on the basis of rationality, in the light of the professional assessments made by JTAC and the Security Service and police.

In logic, he is perfectly right about this. The trouble is that in the public's mind there clearly *is* a link between the WMD issue and intelligence gained by the Security Service or Special Branch, even though we are dealing with entirely different branches of British intelligence with entirely different remits and theatres of operation. Lord Carlile of Berriew made this clear in his February 2006 evidence to the Home Affairs Select Committee, as we have already noted:

He [Lord Carlile] also made clear that the lack of public trust in the security and intelligence services over the terrorist threat stemmed directly from the way the government made the case for war in Iraq: 'The trust issue has been very damaged by the intelligence information connected with the Iraq war which is perceived, rightly or wrongly, to be inaccurate,' he said.[22]

David Omand, however, added a reassuring point – for the record. Having pointed out that Britain did not invade Iraq because of specific pieces of bad intelligence, he suggested they illuminated broader issues that needed attention:

The problems behind those faulty reports and their assessment was dissected by Butler and sensible corrective recommendations made. I oversaw their implementation. So those problems are patently not a big issue now. The future of Iraq is the issue.

For Omand, the overall policy context of the WMD issue was vital:

The causes of the war must be looked for in the change of attitudes in government in the US and UK after 9/11 when the vulnerability of modern urban life, including in future to

WMD, was revealed and highlighted. A stand had to be taken against WMD seen in that context. Iraq happened to be the country in serious long-term violation of international law (UN Resolutions) over a long time. British forces were risking their lives patrolling the no-fly zone over Iraq. Sanctions regimes were loosening and might not be sustainable. Off the sanctions leash Saddam would quickly build WMD; on that, British intelligence assessments were shown to be accurate by the Iraq Survey Group.

He was equally insistent that the war against Iraq was *not*, at its core, about intelligence, secret or otherwise, but about a high-policy decision made after 9/11. He said:

> The Iraq story is a simple one: post 9/11 Washington and London started to wake up. The biggest danger would be a terrorist with a nuclear weapon and something needed to be done about it. The Americans resolved that Iraq was the place to start to deal with the threat because it was a persistent offender against UN resolutions and because it was believed to be a serial WMD offender.

However, even if secret intelligence was not the chief trigger for war, it was the prime minister's choice to make secret intelligence the cornerstone of his political case for war. Bearing in mind that the intelligence was quite wrong, and considering its significance in policy-making, should he have used the 'higher authority' of the intelligence community to justify the attack on Iraq? Ann Taylor believed he was right to do so:

> The blanket view – that the Agencies must be protected – is quite important, but the public these days are so much more aware that the questions should be asked and will be asked about what the Agencies believe is necessary. Ministers can stonewall. In fact, they should give us as full an answer as possible.

WAS THE ISC SUSCEPTIBLE TO POLITICAL PRESSURE?

If the ISC did pull its punches in its 2004–05 report, could it have been that it believed, in an election year in particular, that it should say nothing that might personally embarrass the prime minister who had appointed them? Or could it have been that the chair, Ann Taylor, was reluctant to criticize the leader of her own party? Many will feel that such suggestions are out of order, but we felt compelled to ask Tom King, David Omand, Ann Taylor and other senior interlocutors whether they felt the ISC could be subject to political pressure and, in the case of Ann Taylor, whether the imminence of the 2005 general election had resulted in a sub-standard 2004–05 report. Naturally, the formal fact of dissolution was not known to the ISC when the report was published, but it could count backwards from the generally assumed election date like anyone else.

Ann Taylor soundly rebutted either proposition. She said the ISC had asked itself late in 2004:

> Did they write a report early because it was due later that year or did they risk letting the ISC be overtaken by events – namely a general election?

She added that the ISC began work on its report

> …knowing it would not be a full year and that the report would have to be ready by March. If it had not been an election year, they would have had another three months to work on it. More reports were being written by 2005 – two per annum – previously it had been just one annual one.

(This is an interesting perception on her part, but one that is not actually correct: in fact, the third Committee's overall output was slightly *lower* than that of its two predecessors – in addition to the statutorily required annual report, it produced three 'one-off' reports in four years, as against five 'one-off' reports in just over six years for the King-chaired committees.)

She further pointed out that that her Committee's final report should not be condemned because it is short:

> It is futile to count words in a report – this does not tell you how effective the ISC was.

In one crucial area, however, the ISC did say it was 'disappointed' with the way in which Blair's government used intelligence to make policy. It was an institutional point, and highlighted what it saw as a severe flaw in governance – one that illuminated the propensity of the Blair administration to pursue a presidential style of rule (although it did not couch its criticism in quite those terms!).

This was its persistent failure over the years to convene meetings of the Ministerial Committee on the Intelligence Services (CSI), which had not met since December 2003. That meeting had itself been the first meeting of the committee in *seven* years. There is usually only one reason for avoiding committees, and that is to avoid limiting the power of those who ultimately must exercise it. This was a real rebuke, but lacked strength. It seemed to be a 'Yes, Minister' issue, of little concern to the wider public. Nor is 'disappointed' a particularly strong word to use in the context.

Tom King stressed the status of the ISC in its first few years:

> John Major had set it up and showed considerable respect for it. He put into it five senior members of his party – in particular myself and Lord Howe.

He contrasted this with the initial reaction of the new Labour administration in the years after 1997:

> The ISC was a duty that Blair inherited, but he was not as well briefed about it and its work as he might have been. He played it by ear. Now, of course, he has a better understanding. We should not forget that, before becoming PM, Blair had not even had the most junior role in government and that intelligence and defence issues must effectively have been totally new to him. Nor was it a priority. The Cold War was over and intelligence seemed much less important. Now he clearly understands its importance.

For this very reason (showing the importance he attaches to the ISC's remit), Tom King believes that it makes sense for the chair of the ISC *always* to be a member of the main opposition party:

> Today the chair seems to be a consolation prize for being thrown out of the Cabinet. It is, however, in the prime minister's interest that the ISC be seen to be completely independent. This means the chair should be a member of the Opposition.

King noted sardonically that he himself fulfilled this requirement – the second time round. Yet he doubted that Blair would go for this:

> It obviously does not fit easily with the No. 10 control mentality, and it is a convenient position to have when moving people out of the government.

He accepted that the present ISC chair, Paul Murphy, had 'some track record in the field, from his days in Northern Ireland'. But he suggested that an opposition figure might permit the ISC to bare its teeth more convincingly.

Ann Taylor, perhaps understandably, rejects this view entirely. She herself would presumably have had some experience of working with the Security Service from her time as government chief whip (1997–2001). She stated that, as ISC chair, she had always been entirely independent and by no means 'the prime minister's creature'; to claim otherwise would be 'total nonsense'. She added that, even if she had been inclined to be so – which she was not – her Committee members were senior people:

> It is inconceivable to imagine members like Alan Beith or James Arbuthnot would allow the independence of the Committee to be undermined.

It was, however, true that, from 2001 to 2005, the political importance of the Committee had increased greatly. She

> ...could recall when debates on the ISC were used as 'fillers' when the government wanted a quiet Parliamentary day. There would never be enough speakers – it was an everyday event from the government's point of view. However, from 2001–05 this was never the case.

She added (as we have already noted in Chapter 2), to dispel any final doubts that she might feel a residual loyalty to Tony Blair: 'I had been sacked by him from the perfect job, why should I be in his thrall?' Nor, she insists, did she 'take my cue either from whether there were grudges I might bear or whether there were issues of loyalty to the PM'. She had not asked for the job; initially she had been sceptical about accepting it. In the event she was appointed in the July before 9/11, but was soon 'plunged into reality, regardless of any personal feelings'. Having said that, she added that she was 'loyal' to Blair's government, but not mindlessly so – 'but then again I had just been sacked'.

As to the suggestion put forward by Tom King that the ISC chair should always be a member of the main opposition party, Ann Taylor disagreed:

> This is not a strong position. In fact, being a member of the governing party simply means you have to bend over backwards to be impartial.

We therefore have it on the authority of the first two ISC chairs that over a period of 10-plus years there were no attempts, either direct or indirect, to exert political pressure on the Committee in order that it should temper its judgements on sensitive issues. But this invites the question of whether the ISC itself had a corporate reluctance to dig deep and criticize harshly. It is certainly not helpful to the ISC's case that the leaders of the two main opposition parties in the UK did not trust it to deliver the sort of review that Lord Butler went on to provide. Yet even Butler, who obtained greater access to information on intelligence sources than the ISC ever has, felt compelled to couch his criticisms of the government and the Agencies in the most mandarin of terms. If the ISC did pull its punches, that could be due to traditional British reserve; or it could be that, over the years, the Committee had got too close to the Agencies – becoming their supporters rather than their overseers – a possibility we go on to explore now.

WAS THE ISC TOO CLOSE TO THE AGENCIES?

All secret agencies have a quasi-mythical status that they exploit to full effect, not least as a tool in recruiting staff and agents. Their leaders can be charismatic individuals with a degree of mystique (the head of SIS is known, for example, as 'C' and to this day signs himself as such in green ink). All of this gives agency chiefs a considerable amount of authority; were the members of the ISC in awe of it? Did it cause them to pull their punches? Were they effectively co-opted into the system through their top-secret briefings and their privileged membership of the 'ring of secrecy'?

Ann Taylor recognized the theoretical possibility of this but denied vehemently that it happens in practice. In the early days of the ISC she believed that, yes, 'agency heads could get away with this sort of thing'. By the time she became chair, however, the ISC had already gained good experience of dealing with the Agencies, at one level or another. Indeed, some had contact with the Agencies prior to joining the ISC. Ann Taylor said that she would not wish to be specific on this issue, but that

> Joyce Quin, James Arbuthnot, Alan Beith, Michael Mates all brought something of their experiences to the ISC.

In her experience,

> [the agency heads] were more frank with the ISC than with ministers. Had I stayed in office I might have improved this – but of course I cannot be sure – but I did make progress here.

As evidence of this, she cited the work done by her Committee on Bali and WMD, which was 'high-profile work', as well as work on 'other areas on which I cannot comment where real progress was also made, which likewise cannot be mentioned'. She believed that ministers would readily 'acknowledge that the ISC had brought things to their attention of which they were not previously fully aware'.

Ann Taylor's views were echoed by David Omand. He pointed out that the members of the ISC since Tom King's days would

> ...meet with agency heads in a peculiarly British compromise, delivering something that they did not get otherwise in terms of trust between the intelligence world and the ISC.

This rested, he said,

> ...on the belief that the ISC understands what it does – why secrecy is necessary, to have some respect for the risks the Agencies and their staff and agents have to face.

The ISC had shown it understood the point:

> Increasingly the ISC has been taken into the confidence of the Agencies in the things that go on – it is briefed off the record by heads and senior officials to enable it to make sense of what has happened when there are major developments or in terms of future issues such as information security and cyberwar.

None of this, he said, was laid down in the statute that established the ISC. Rather it was the outcome of the way in which Tom King described the Committee's development:

> The ISC is an incremental committee, in the sense that its remit has grown, has expanded to meet needs the ISC has identified. It is located, perhaps, between two extremes – say the US one and the French one. At one stage, the Inspector General of the CIA had a staff of around 140. In addition both the Senate and the House have their intelligence oversight committees with substantial staffs...The French system of parliamentary oversight is virtually non-existent.

He recalled:

> As a new Committee, the ISC developed its oversight as it went along, and extended its coverage significantly. Three particular developments were significant. First, the DIS were not included

in the original legislative remit of the ISC but were clearly an integral part of the intelligence community and the Committee took a keen interest in its work.

Secondly, King said, the Committee had come to realize that it needed the assistance of the National Audit Office in its scrutiny of the Agencies' finances:

> Initially the way they were presented was totally inadequate. The Intelligence Vote was cloaked in total secrecy and not subject to parliamentary oversight at all, although the chair of the Public Accounts Committee was shown some figures. Asterisks are shown in the ISC reports, but the actual figures are seen by the ISC, down to such details as the total payments to agents. It is important to realize that the legislation never instructed the ISC to do any of this. But it insisted it be done, and it believed it was a helpful process for the Agencies to see figures presented in a different way from the Whitehall standard.

Indeed, Tom King maintained that the public could know far more about the actual sums involved. At the same time, he warned that

> …it is important not to send signals to our enemies as to what we are investing in operations and so on. Some things are truly sensitive and must be kept secret.

The third development, in his view, was the appointment of an ISC Investigator, to which we return below.

We have found no evidence that either the chair or the members of the ISC were, in fact, seduced by the glamour of the intelligence world, the kudos attaching to the UK Agencies, or the personal charm of the agency heads. Yet, as we shall see, we do have one concrete example where it does appear that the ISC's wish to maintain a comfortable relationship with the Agencies and avoid a showdown influenced its decision making, namely in its treatment of its own Investigator, John Morrison.

Once again, if the ISC is to be truly effective, it must not kow-tow to the agency chiefs any more than to the prime minister of the day. Of course, it must not wilfully seek conflict or alienate those with whom it has to work. But cooperation with those who possess great power is not the end in itself of the ISC's work, simply the means to that end. And, from time to time, the ISC needs to show that it has teeth and that it, and not agency heads or government ministers, calls the shots.

HOW IS THE ISC'S WORK REGARDED FROM *WITHIN* WHITEHALL?

David Omand has pointed out:

> Unlike most other countries' oversight bodies, the ISC is not there to oversee operational matters – it is a committee of parliamentarians (Lords and Commons) to oversee the efficiency and administration of the secret services. Ever since it was set up, it has in practice been shifting the boundaries – Tom King was the important figure here – without taking matters to the point where HMG would have to re-legislate.

However, David Omand maintained that Ann Taylor, rather than Tom King, was mainly responsible for expanding the ISC's remit in practice, with the government's agreement, so that the Committee's effective cover included

> …the Cabinet Office Assessments Staff, the JIC and [it reached a] concordat with MoD for the oversight of the relevant parts of the DIS. None of this was thought about when Statute was introduced, but is working well and was supported by Lord Butler's Committee. I supported this move for it gives the ISC a rounded view of the world of intelligence, especially in support of military operations.

The important thing, he insisted, is that

> HMG and the secret Agencies have accepted this. HMG have found it useful, e.g. the Bali bombing, to satisfy the public that nothing had been missed. The Agencies have found it useful to have an authoritative group of parliamentarians properly briefed on their role and organization, given the amount of misinformation the subject attracts in the media, and have built up a relationship of confidence with the ISC (the 'ring of secrecy') and could see the value of an independent view being expressed to the PM as well as to the public. For the latter, it is vital to the Agencies that they are able to advise the ISC on any redactions in their reports on security grounds. Formally, the reports are to the PM, who could insist on deletions, but

in practice the ISC has been satisfied with the Agencies' explanations of why certain details should be asterisked in the final reports.

On the formal status of the Committee, he commented:

> This aspect of the relationship works because the ISC reports to the prime minister – if it were a select committee then it would make its own rules with the authority of Parliament and, as with other select committees, could choose to publish details on the authority of Parliament or bring in outside advisors, etc., even if the Agencies and therefore the government had reservations. All this helps to build trust, and the Agencies are very conscious they must not overstep the mark and must justify any security concerns they have.

Should the ISC be a select committee? Ann Taylor dismissed the idea with considerable scorn:

> This is one of the futile debates on which people get hung up. The ground rules would be the same if it was the ISC or a select committee in any case because not anyone could walk into its deliberations. One has got to operate within the ring of secrecy. However, it might be possible to have a parliamentary vote to endorse the actual membership of the ISC. That would constitute a simple way forward.

In her view there are no advantages in select committees, and any change in structure would knock back the frankness of the Agencies vis-à-vis the Committee:

> Indeed, the attitudes of those giving evidence has changed dramatically. It is now totally different in volume and quality to what had been provided during my early tenure. The ISC is now told more, and told it more quickly. Any structural change would set back the work of the Committee.

David Omand agreed, though he noted:

> We did debate long and hard as to whether the ISC should be another select committee and we agreed that, even if they simply reported directly back to Parliament, the potential loss would outweigh the gain. The ISC itself therefore has, under Tom King and Ann Taylor, opposed strongly becoming a select committee. Such a change would require legislation and there is

no appetite anywhere for that. It therefore continues to report directly to the PM. In fact, it has always been the PM who has been seen by Parliament as ultimately accountable for the overall intelligence community, even if the statutory duty of accountability for individual Agencies lies with the Secretary of State for Foreign Affairs (SIS and GCHQ) and the Home Secretary (the Security Service).

We now turn to some of the issues addressed by the ISC in its latest (2004–05) annual report, as well as in others from earlier years.

REFORMING THE INTELLIGENCE MACHINERY OF GOVERNMENT

As we have noted, in its 2004–05 annual report, the ISC did not focus on the *politics* of the intelligence-led line being taken on Iraq. Rather, it homed in on the *machinery* of the intelligence community – the personnel and the systems used by the government to ensure the efficient operation of Britain's intelligence community. In particular, it drew attention to the central – and critical – role played by the Security and Intelligence Co-ordinator and, it seemed, were satisfied with both the job and the person filling it (they were referring to David Omand, who retired in March 2005).

In its 2004–05 report, the ISC also undertook a review of the progress in implementing the recommendations on professional practice that Lord Butler had made. In doing so, it reported that previous SIS procedures had, in several respects, been inadequate, and that SIS was, in effect, reverting to its previous quality-control system, with a senior SIS officer appointed to check the accuracy of SIS's products, distancing those involved with operations from those involved in reporting.[23] The Committee noted that the Butler Committee recommendations were

> ...in the process of being fully implemented. These are important changes and we will comment in due course on their implementation and to what extent they are appropriate and effective.[24]

It should be noted here that the ISC was fully aware that it was about to be disbanded prior to the general election, and that the 'we' in the quote could only refer to its successors. But, in concluding in these terms, the Committee was effectively binding the new post-election membership to a commitment it would be hard, if not impossible, to evade.

THE WAR ON TERROR

We have already commented on the Committee's unfortunate (in hindsight) statement in the introduction to its 2004–05 report that

> …**we wish to place on record our appreciation of the staff within the UK Intelligence Community. Without their work, the UK would not have been protected against terrorist attack.** [emphasis in original]

Some might argue that it would be facile to criticize the ISC for its failure to foresee that there would be a new manifestation of the terrorist threat – networks of home-grown Islamist suicide bombers – which the Security Service itself did not regard as a pressing problem. Yet, in its 2004–05 report, the ISC made a specific point of insisting that the terror threat within the UK emanated from *individuals* and not networks, stating in paragraph 5:

> It is impossible to quantify exactly the number of individuals within the UK associated with Islamic [*sic*] terrorism…We have been told by the Director General that, in a significant proportion of the cases of suspected terrorism-related activity investigated by the Security Service, there is credible intelligence of involvement in such activity. The need to address the threat from these individuals is the primary reason why the Security Service is currently expanding significantly and the Agencies have been provided with additional funding.

Securing the UK from terrorism was, by 2004–05, very obviously at the forefront of the ISC's collective mind; it stated that the 'general threats to the UK' were both 'real and current'.[25] Nor was the war on terror a new concern for the ISC: ever since 1994 (when the ISC was formed) it had been a subject in which it had taken a consistent interest. However, with the passage of time, its significance had increased steadily. By 2005, the threat to Britain from 'Islamic terrorist groups' ('global in its nature and reach') was 'ever present'[26] and therefore highly dangerous. British citizens were being killed outside the UK, even though, as the ISC had to concede, it was still not possible to quantify exactly the number of individuals within the UK associated with Islamist terrorism.[27]

The ISC pointed out that, since 10 September 2001, over one hundred UK nationals had been murdered by Al Qaeda or groups associated with it.[28] Despite the criticisms of the British intelligence community that were outlined in its 2004–05 report, the ISC declared emphatically that overall the secret Agencies had done 'excellent work' for Britain, without which we would not have been 'protected against terrorist attack'. The British public could be reassured, the ISC claimed, that the Security Service was working closely with the police and other agencies to 'identify and investigate UK nationals and residents who are willing to undertake terrorist activity'.[29] Yet 'The Threat' section of the 2004–05 annual report[30] covers terrorism in only three paragraphs – less than a page – compared with nine paragraphs and two pages on the Agencies' relationship with the media.[31]

Ann Taylor has said, however, that she would be amazed if any intelligence professional were to argue that no one was expecting UK suicide bombers to act in Britain:

> In one of our earlier reports we said the perspective had changed since 9/11; this showed there were extremists with the audacity and willingness to die. This had altered the threat assessment; Sarin, various explosives – it would not take much to act in this way. However the day, the time and the place was a surprise, but that it happened did not take me by surprise. One of my former constituents was a ringleader.

Perhaps her Committee's last report could have made this point more forcibly; as it was, the lay reader could be excused for thinking, as we have already noted, that the terrorist threat was essentially under control. The report (and indeed its predecessors) might also have highlighted the effects of the Security Service's 1992 decision to cease operating against subversion – a point to which we shall return.

Clearly, it was going to be impossible to forecast the London attacks without predictive intelligence. Yet this intelligence was only to be gained if the terrorists slipped up in some way (which could not be counted on) or if subversive and potential terrorist networks had been successfully penetrated by the Security Service.

Asked whether it had been a mistake to stop operating against subversion, Ann Taylor declined to comment on that specific issue, but went on to make a general point about the public perception of intelligence 'failures':

> I cannot speak about this matter [subversion] but I wish this issue had got into the public domain. There is a really good chapter on this in Butler, dealing with the nature and limitations of intelligence. One of the things we have all got a responsibility for is to make people understand the nature of the difficulties that the Agencies face. People use the word 'failure' in a glib way. There is a finite amount that is knowable and if only they worked harder to find it, there might be more successes. For this reason, I resent those who perpetuate the myth of failure. In public terms this has got to be got over.

Her comments are perfectly fair, and the term 'failure' should not be used in a glib manner; but surely it was part and parcel of the ISC's duties to 'get this issue into the public domain earlier'. It did not do so.

Was it not an obvious failure to square up to the implications of SIS's discovery of WMD that did not exist? Ann Taylor rejected this charge in its totality:

> The idea that Saddam had WMD was not fantasy. Everyone believed it. There was a need to get this issue in perspective so the ISC looked back to 1990. It was not just an SIS issue and the ISC made some very significant comments about this which were followed up by Butler and have led to changes in procedure. This was something that was not covered before my time. The cuts and the impact they had after the Cold War had not been looked at before the ISC did so. The *raison d'être* created by the Cold War had been lost when it ended.

Her last point is, of course, entirely correct, but, once again, it is a shame it was not made explicit in this report.

COMMUNITY MATTERS

Much of the 2004–05 report is taken up with the machinery of the intelligence community – pages 7–17 investigate issues such as the work of the Security and Intelligence Co-ordinator, the DIS, JIC and Assessments Staff, agency expenditure and resources, and administration. 'Policy' (four pages) looks only at joint working and the efficiency advisor, and vetting. Iraqi WMD is covered in a bare three pages. The Butler review, SCOPE (the intelligence community's web-based information system), work on economic well-being and on serious and organized crime take up a further seven pages, and legislation – the Official Secrets Act and intercept as evidence – another two.

In taking a detailed look at these aspects of the machinery of intelligence, the ISC was, of course, doing no more than meeting its statutory requirement to examine the 'expenditure, administration and policy' of the Agencies. But it is remarkable how little of the third Committee's final report is devoted to the intelligence issues of substantive concern to Parliament and the public. One is left with the impression that its members had rather lost heart, and that a workmanlike but uncontroversial report was the best they could manage.

WORKING WITH THE MEDIA

However, during 2004–05 the ISC did tackle a new subject: the ways in which the Agencies worked together with the media, and the process by which certain journalists could gain accreditation. While this could appear a progressive and enlightened move in favour of transparency, it had, of course, a downside that the ISC did not mention: that these chosen few were laying themselves open to the charge that they were stooges of the intelligence services.[32] We consider later in this chapter an earlier example of how intelligence/media relationships can go very wrong.

THE COMMITTEE SPEAKS OUT ON SOME ISSUES...

Reading between the lines of the 2004–05 ISC report, the 'governance of intelligence' issues that the outgoing Committee felt obliged to address could be read as signalling that reform of at least some parts of the British intelligence community was needed. Some of the systemic problems were demonstrated by the handling of intelligence on Iraqi WMD.

There was no suggestion in what the ISC wrote that the prime minister or the foreign secretary had done anything other than react in a proper fashion to the secret intelligence on WMD with which they were presented – no evidence, for example, that they had ordered intelligence to be manufactured. Yet it was plain that neither man possessed sufficient expertise to question the accuracy of this intelligence. Nor, apparently, did either have sufficient understanding of the nature of intelligence to appreciate the point that what they were being told about was not just far more 'raw' than they might have been led to believe, but had not yet been passed to the acknowledged experts in the field, the Defence Intelligence Staff

(DIS), for verification. And, in the case of the prime minister, there was an almost messianic determination to present intelligence as holy writ, which it would be virtually blasphemous for Parliament or public to question.

The ISC, therefore, identified problems within the intelligence community affecting both collection (SIS) and analysis (JIC), even if it was reluctant to say so directly in its final report. It is also clear from the 2004–05 report that there were serious flaws in the systems and processes by which intelligence was fed into the policy-making machine in 10 Downing Street and the Foreign and Commonwealth Office. In particular, the ISC detailed the constantly changing duties given to the government's most important intelligence advisors since 1995 and the unwillingness to construct a system for building intelligence assessments into the time-honoured and long-established practices of Cabinet government.

…BUT IS STRANGELY SILENT ON ONE

Before moving on from the ISC's 2004–05 report, we should note a peculiar omission. It concerns the fate of John Morrison, the ISC Investigator, an appointment whose origins were described in Chapter 2. John Morrison (one of the authors of this book), a former deputy chief of defence intelligence, and by then an independent consultant on intelligence and security issues, was selected for this part-time position in 1999. By 2000 he had looked at the Agencies' security policies and procedures and reported on their IT systems and policies, and was, at the time, investigating the UK's intelligence and security oversight system (which he found to be functioning well enough), and recruitment, retention and career development in the Agencies. By 2001, his work was receiving the highest commendation; he was tasked with examining the scientific and technical research and development supported by the Agencies and went on in subsequent years to investigate a wide range of subjects.

Indeed, in the House of Commons debate on the Committee's 2003–04 annual report, James Arbuthnot commended the work of the ISC support team, including Morrison:

> I want to pay tribute to the Committee's Chairman and Clerk, and to its staff and investigator who have worked extremely hard to help us all.[33]

Three days later, on 11 July 2004, Morrison appeared on the current affairs programme *Panorama* in his capacity as a former deputy chief of defence intelligence who had left the civil service in 1999. At his request, no mention was made of the fact that he worked for the ISC on a contractual basis. However, his criticism of the prime minister, for what he maintained had been an incorrect definition of the supposed 'threat' presented by Iraq, clearly struck a raw nerve with the Agencies. They wrote to the Security and Intelligence Co-ordinator saying that they had lost faith in Morrison, and could no longer work with him.[34] It might have been expected that the ISC would have ignored the Agencies' request. Instead, the ISC decided to terminate Morrison's contract prematurely. There has been no credible suggestion that No. 10 played any part in this, but subsequently the prime minister's official spokesman told the media (incorrectly) that Morrison had not been sacked but that his contract would not be renewed when it expired. In fact, the ISC invoked the clause in Morrison's contract with the Cabinet Office that allowed either side to terminate at 90 days' notice.[35]

It would be hard to argue that the resulting media brouhaha did either the ISC or the government much good. Many pointed out that the only person to have lost a job as a result of the Iraq intelligence fiasco was the one who had publicly dared 'speak truth unto power'. Under the circumstances, it is disappointing, but perhaps not surprising, that the 2004–05 report simply pretended that Morrison did not exist.[36]

Ann Taylor was dismissive of the idea that Morrison had been sacked, claiming rather that the Committee no longer had any need of his services:

> His role had become less central because the work that was central to the Committee was by now so important that it was no longer a case of monitoring the processes of the Agencies, but involved following very important issues such as Bali, Iraq. These were so important that all Committee members had to read all the materials themselves. They did not rely on an Investigator to do it for them, nor did they want to do so.

Be that as it may (and Morrison had already made it clear that he would not be seeking a renewal of his contract when it came to an end in April 2005), the public perception was that the ISC had buckled under pressure from the Agencies. And, *pace* Ann Taylor, it could be argued that, if the ISC was to spend more time on substantive intelligence issues such as Bali and Iraq (a type of subject that the Investigator had never been tasked with exploring), then it had a greater rather than a lesser need for someone who, on their behalf, could dig into the 'machinery of intelligence' issues identified in the 2004–05 report.

WHO GIVES THE PRIME MINISTER INTELLIGENCE ADVICE?

One aspect of this particularly significant question is the strong suspicion that the prime minister had lacked objective and authoritative advice about the secret intelligence on WMD that SIS officers were showing him. In particular, it seems that 'C' had greater access to him than was sensible, given 'C's obvious strengths as a 'salesman' for Humint (even though all three agency heads have access to the PM as of right). The prime minister's chief advisor on substantive intelligence issues would normally be the chairman of the JIC, but it is unclear whether he was able (or indeed disposed) to warn Blair about the dangers of accepting raw intelligence uncritically.

Ann Taylor herself conceded:

> Almost by definition, a prime minister won't know everything about intelligence. This is not a black or white thing. David Omand was perfect for Tony Blair, the perfect individual to have at that place at that time…The fact is that all these relationships depend on individuals and conditions at the time. And one should not cut across agency heads' rights to go to the PM when they think fit.

Yet she concluded somewhat cryptically:

> Tony Blair had plenty of advice. Nothing is definitive, and the policy issue is always different from the intelligence ones.

We therefore have a situation, in both the UK and the USA, where the requirement for good secret intelligence, well-based all-source assessments, sound security policies, and thoughtful advice to the chief policy-maker has probably never been greater, and certainly not in peace time. Yet those charged with producing such inputs appear to have relied overmuch on covert sources, rather than drawing on a full range of sources. In this context, Lord Butler specifically stated that the value of international organizations (such as UNSCOM and the International Atomic Energy Agency (IAEA) in the case of Iraq) needed to be recognized and built on for the future, supported by the contribution of intelligence from national agencies.[37] The Butler Committee also concluded that further steps were needed to integrate the relevant work of the DIS more closely with the rest of the intelligence community.[38]

HOW GOOD IS OVERSIGHT? THE ISC HAS FEW DOUBTS

As to whether the *system* does or does not work, it is, perhaps, not surprising that the ISC itself, in its successive incarnations, appears to have believed that it does. Rather peculiarly, its 2002 brochure *Intelligence Oversight*[39] adduced in evidence of this one specific and rather special media view:

> So does the system work? The *Times* leader on 14 June 2000, the day after the Committee published its report into the handling of Mr Mitrokhin's material, said:

> 'Never before has a Parliamentary Committee been given such access to documents detailing MI5's operations; never has the service been so publicly reprimanded…Yet the report can do nothing but good for Britain's security and intelligence services. For the parliamentary committee has made abundantly clear that not only can it be trusted with some of the most sensitive information in British Intelligence, but that it can produce a report that is thorough, focused, rigorous in identifying individual failings and yet in no way compromising to Britain's security. This, in the end, can only solidify the basis on which the security services operate, and bolster public confidence in the way they are policed. MI5 is rightly smarting at the lapses exposed yesterday; but in the long term it should welcome this strikingly successful example of public accountability…
> The Mitrokhin affair involved a lamentable failure to keep Government informed; Parliament has done well to keep the country informed of that failure.'[40]

What the ISC does not say about *The Times* is that it was hardly a neutral party in the Mitrokhin Affair, having won the race to name the former KGB agent that the Security Service wanted to keep secret – but more on this later. Perhaps more reliable praise came from the Home Affairs Select Committee report, *Accountability of the Security Service*, published in June 1999 and also quoted in the ISC brochure, which stated that

> …the reports of the ISC itself have shed light on areas of security service activity which hitherto had lain in darkness. These developments have been an important advance on what had gone before.[41]

The ISC concluded in its brochure:

> These quotes suggest that the Committee plays a large role in maintaining public confidence in the intelligence and security Agencies, whilst drawing attention to their failings as appropriate. The key element in the Committee's relationship is trust. The Agencies have learned to trust that the Committee is secure and will not leak secrets. This means that they can respond to the Committee and be open without fear of being compromised.
>
> The system of oversight exercised by the ISC has evolved since its establishment in 1994 and it will, without doubt, continue to do so. Oversight of the intelligence and security Agencies is now regarded as an important part of democratic society and any future developments will be based on the foundations created by the ISC.[42]

Ann Taylor has, however, endorsed the need to continue striving for improvements in the oversight system:

> There is no complacency at any level – not with the Agencies, not with No. 10. We have got to make sure we don't have a failure of imagination in terms of anticipating the audacity of people who want to damage society – whether they are motivated by religion or animal rights. We've also got to have, in the JIC, the equivalent of blue skies thinking, to ensure we think the impossible without becoming obsessed. And after all that we have to decide the extent to which we are willing to have our lives encroached upon.

She declined to comment on the fourth and current incarnation of the ISC:

> It is not for me to judge the next Committee. However, a little more continuity would have been desirable. Yet several members of the ISC left Parliament in 2005 and the pool of candidates is not very great. The workload is an exceptional one and all previous members have done their share of it. Had I stayed in the Commons I would have liked to stay on as chair – it was the one pull I had – even if I hadn't known what I would be taking on. Yet attendance in my time was almost one hundred per cent.

Ann Taylor staunchly refuted the argument that the ISC pulls its punches:

> There is a natural progression in the work of any committee – the relevance of the ISC increased after 9/11, and the issues which it covered became much more centre stage. The reports did not pull their punches, they were quite frank reports and our approach was always straightforward. Getting unanimous reports from individuals, all of whom had a high degree of credibility, was an achievement. The ISC was a very serious committee, all pulled their weight. Agreement is hard to get, but it was achieved; all did their homework and read all the documentation and attended all the meetings. I did not know of any more hard-working committee in all my time in Parliament.

Despite these fine efforts, it is questionable whether the British people retain, in the words of the ISC's brochure, complete 'public confidence in the intelligence and security Agencies', even to the extent that it may have existed even in July 2002. At the same time, the point that 'oversight is now regarded as an important part of democratic society' and that the ISC has established itself cannot be denied. Yet the Committee's belief in its own excellence must inevitably contain an element of Panglossian optimism – would it not have been better if the ISC had at least *appeared* to be more self-critical? This is not, however, a major problem, and we now move on to some more trenchant questions.

THE 'RING OF SECRECY' AND THE CONCEPT OF 'OVERSIGHT'

The biggest questions have to do with two rather deeper but interrelated quasi-constitutional concerns. The first is about the political consequences stemming from the obligation of the ISC to work within the 'ring of secrecy'. The second is about the constitutional location of 'oversight' within what the ISC interestingly identifies as 'democratic society' – a much looser concept than 'parliamentary liberal democracy' and, one presumes, one chosen for this very reason.

The phrase 'ring of secrecy' is found in the very first publication of the ISC.[43] In outlining its statutory responsibilities, Tom King stated that its work would involve the examination of

> ...the expenditure, administration and policy of the UK's three intelligence and security Agencies: SIS, GCHQ and the Security Service

adding that

> [b]ecause of the nature of the Committee's work, it must have access to national security information and Committee members therefore have all been notified under the Official Secrets Act 1989. We are now operating within the 'ring of secrecy', reporting directly to you [the prime minister] on our work and *through you* to Parliament. [our emphasis]

The notion that the ISC should be required to work within the 'ring of secrecy' immediately raised questions about the nature and significance of its work. How is oversight played out? Is it located in the act of presenting ISC reports to the prime minister? Or is the act of 'oversight' consummated by the publication of the sanitized ISC reports to Parliament? If it is the first of these, why does ISA 1994 require the prime minister to lay sanitized copies of the ISC's annual reports before each House of Parliament? If it is not, and oversight consists in Parliament being presented with the reports, why give it first to the chief intelligence policy-maker (the prime minister), but offer Parliament (and through it the public) an incomplete version?

Working as they do within the 'ring of secrecy' and intimately involved with the players in the UK intelligence community, the Committee appears at times to be attempting to square the circle of supporting the intelligence Agencies and criticizing aspects of their behaviour. When the ISC states that it 'strongly supports the work of the Security Service', for example, what exactly is this meant to imply? On one level, it is a banal statement of the obvious (which upright citizen would not support the work of the Security Service?). On another, however, it could be read as suggesting that it is enough for the Security Service to satisfy the ISC for its work to be deemed supportable. This matter was first addressed head-on in the 2001–02 ISC annual report (the first one produced by the new chair, Ann Taylor). She wrote:

> The Committee has been impressed by the Agencies' work during the period covered by this report...While this Report will highlight the areas about which the Committee has concerns, *as that is the purpose of oversight*, it must not overshadow the tremendous efforts made by the Agencies'

staff sometimes at great personal risk, to gain valuable secret intelligence for the UK. This intelligence safeguards national security, economic wellbeing and it helps prevent and detect serious organised crime. It significantly reduces the threat to the UK and its citizens.[44] [our emphasis]

Is it therefore the case that 'oversight' means no more than collecting the 'concerns' picked up by a group of worthy parliamentarians in their examination of the work of the intelligence community on a relatively ad hoc basis; and that once these concerns have been expressed to the prime minister, and then, in sanitized form, to Parliament, oversight has been completed? Or should it be more than this? Should it consist of a systematic and in-depth probing of intelligence policy and practice, and the formulation of quite specific proposals, which the government should either accept or reject at its peril? The work of the National Audit Office in this regard is well worth bearing in mind.

The answers to these questions have changed over time, and are likely to change yet again in the aftermath of the Iraqi WMD debacle and the July 2005 terrorist attacks on London. The concept of 'oversight' is obviously subject to alteration and adaptation and, in several respects, a genuine refinement of oversight can be seen to have taken place. Even so, the true location of 'oversight' in the UK remains somewhat mysterious; ten years on, it still appears to reside somewhere in the no-man's-land between the prime minister, the ministers responsible for the Agencies, the individuals and bodies charged with overseeing specific aspects of the Agencies' work,[45] and the ISC. If the government decides it dislikes a particular Committee recommendation or request, it is at perfect liberty to ignore it (as it frequently has) and proceed as though all were well, thus demonstrating the limits on the effectiveness of intelligence oversight in the UK system.

EXAMINING AGENCY POLICIES AND PRACTICES

In 1994–95 Tom King, echoing the terms of ISA 1994, spoke about the ISC's need to examine the 'policy' of the secret Agencies.[46] In constitutional theory, at any rate, it might seem surprising to learn that Britain's secret Agencies produce their own policies, rather than follow the policy of the government as set down in the national intelligence requirements. But while it is true that the Agencies exist to implement government policy, it is equally true that they need to generate and implement their own internal 'policies' in order to carry out their responsibilities on a day-to-day basis. At times, however, they may need to undertake 'strategic' policy initiatives on a scale requiring government approval. An example of this was the move within a decade of all three Agencies into new headquarters (SIS and the Security Service in 1995, GCHQ in 2004), each requiring large capital investment involving central funding that had to be authorized by the Treasury.

The only agency which could be said to have its own 'policy' when it comes to setting an agenda is the Security Service (although even the Security Service has to take note of the government's national intelligence requirements), since its activities are in reaction to threats it itself identifies. However, the overall agenda for the work of the Agencies is (or is meant to be) firmly set by the government. Ever since the 1970s, fears have existed in some quarters (especially among Labour politicians, the media and academic commentators) that 'rogue elements' might be using the power of the secret Agencies to follow their own policies, and even to plot against the government of the day.[47] To date, however, the ISC has found absolutely no evidence that the Agencies have had goals independent of those of the government, or in conflict with them, although, as we shall see, eyebrows were raised (and knuckles rapped) in respect of some of the Security Service's decisions. Yet, as we demonstrated in detail earlier, none was unconstitutional.

Other issues emerging over time, but also stemming from the need to act within the 'ring of secrecy', are not difficult to identify. The ISC increasingly probes into very detailed matters of agency activity. This raises the question as to whether parliamentarians, even those with direct ministerial experience of the Agencies, possess sufficient knowledge and expertise to analyse properly the judgements or actions of intelligence professionals. If the best judges of professional intelligence activity are intelligence professionals, then it is hard to see the purpose of a committee composed of politicians (even those said to have 'relevant' experience).[48] How 'relevant' is 'relevant'? Is a widely respected elder statesman and former secretary of state (Tom King, who held five S of S posts, including Northern Ireland and defence) more useful in an oversight role than a less prominent politician but former military intelligence officer (Michael Mates)? Is a former ministerial acquaintance with the intelligence community as a customer or overseer the best qualification for parliamentary duties in this field? There are probably no correct or final answers to these questions, but there may well have been too much that was 'ad hoc' in what the ISC does and too little long-term strategic planning.

In addition to examining the machinery of intelligence, the ISC's work has increasingly meant that it has been presented with substantive intelligence assessments, both oral (as in the run-up to the invasion of Iraq) and written (as in its examination of JIC papers on Iraqi WMD). But is this strictly necessary for a body whose statutory responsibilities do not require it to address assessed intelligence? This is an important matter to which we shall return, because it could be argued either that the ISC is acting *ultra vires* in accepting such assessments at face value, or that the critical scrutiny of assessments is a legitimate oversight function that is being executed in an inconsistent and amateur manner.

The ISC has undertaken a fair amount of foreign travel: its annual reports show a steady stream of overseas tours, as well as incoming visits by foreign counterparts. To some, this could smack of 'jollies' for Committee members, but the ISC would surely be failing in its duties if it did not keep up with oversight developments abroad and pass on its experience to other countries, notably those where intelligence oversight is comparatively new. The ISC has also participated in successive International Intelligence Review Agencies conferences, hosting the May 2002 meeting in London. Thus, international contacts provide a way for the Committee both to learn and to teach.

THE ISC: KEY CONSTITUTIONAL AND MANAGEMENT ISSUES

As we have already noted in considering the 2004–05 annual report, one issue that the ISC came to grapple with increasingly (though it reached no clear conclusion) was the question of who advised the prime minister on the strength of the intelligence he was being offered. The very fact that this was a process that was continually being tinkered with can be seen as a cause for concern, suggesting as it does that there was no clear vision of the relationship between the Agencies, the JIC, the Cabinet Office and the prime minister. This lack of clarity is identified both in the ISC's reports and in that of the Butler Committee.

The ISC's 2003–04 annual report says that, since David Omand's appointment as Security and Intelligence Co-ordinator,

[he] is now effectively the Prime Minister's advisor on security and intelligence-related matters, a task he has taken over from the Cabinet Secretary.

At the same time, the ISC report made it clear that, despite his membership of the JIC, Omand was not an advisor on substantive intelligence matters:

> It is not his role to advise the Prime Minister on the available intelligence or the assessments. That is the job of the JIC Chairman.[49]

David Omand served as Security and Intelligence Co-ordinator until March 2005, when he took early retirement, to be replaced by Bill Jeffrey, formerly director general of the Immigration and Nationality Directorate in the Home Office. Jeffrey's tenure was brief, however, for on 29 September 2005 it was announced that Sir Richard Mottram, permanent secretary at the Department of Work and Pensions, was to take over as Security and Intelligence Co-ordinator, and would also become chairman of the Joint Intelligence Committee (JIC), with Jeffrey becoming permanent secretary of the MoD. Mottram's appointment met Butler's recommendation that the post of chairman of the JIC should be held by someone 'with experience of dealing with Ministers in a very senior role, and who is demonstrably beyond influence, and thus probably in his [sic] last post'.[50] Richard Mottram clearly met that requirement, having served in the most senior civil service positions for over ten years and being well known (indeed notorious) for plain speaking to ministers.

Speaking to us, David Omand clarified the relationship between himself, the chairman of the JIC and the prime minister:

> The role which I took up in September 2002 as Security and Intelligence Co-ordinator in respect of intelligence (there were other roles in respect of homeland security) was that of strategic planning, coordination and finance (as Accounting Officer for the Single Intelligence Account), essentially doing what previously the Cabinet secretary had done. My authority was derived from the Cabinet secretary, and through him to the PM. I was not a member of the prime minister's staff in No. 10. I was the line manager of the chair of the JIC, but it was part of the terms of appointment that the chair of the JIC would report directly to the PM on the content of intelligence assessment,

and the Co-ordinator would not seek to substitute his judgement for that of the chair of the JIC.

I rejoined the JIC when I was appointed Co-ordinator, having previously been on it as MoD Policy Director and then Director GCHQ – seven years' JIC service in all. I had the opportunity, as a member of the JIC, to inject views and debate the intelligence assessments, but in the end it is the collective view of the JIC that counts.

These changes allowed the Cabinet secretary to concentrate on civil service reform, and allowed me to build a totally new approach to integrated UK homeland security, as well as look after and represent the intelligence community and policy. It was the chair of the JIC whose job it was to act as arbiter of conflicting intelligence judgements.

He added that the appointment of Richard Mottram as Co-ordinator *and* as chairman of the JIC had changed the previous position and produced a unified structure that had been lacking.

David Omand was insistent that, if there were problems with the intelligence over Iraq, they were not the outcome of a confused structure within Downing Street or No. 10:

There was no muddle over the flow of intelligence to No. 10, just an occasional glitch which is bound to happen with the pace of events. The system is that no intelligence goes to the PM which the chair of the JIC has not seen; usually also, if very significant, it was copied to me for information.

He reminded us that the role of Intelligence Co-ordinator had been created in the 1960s (in fact in 1968, with Sir Dick White being the first incumbent) to provide a wise senior figure to help the Cabinet secretary. The government used the post to sort out quarrels over turf and budgets and to look at future trends. It had become largely an honorific role, filled by able people who had active agency experience and knew their way around, but who would not make waves or see themselves as being in charge of the intelligence community.

With David Omand's appointment, in his words

...the intention was to have a senior PUS taking on the role who had had policy experience as well as having worked with the intelligence community. I had run an Agency, been Policy

Director of MoD and the PUS of the Home Office, so was uniquely qualified to set the job up. It coincided with the need to build up 'homeland security' and develop a long-term counter-terrorist strategy for the UK, and these were the areas that I concentrated on. The setting up of JTAC was, for example, a big step. The fact that JTAC did not foresee 7/7 should not damn the concept – there was no intelligence that would have enabled pre-emption. But although 7/7 came as a tactical surprise, it was not a strategic surprise: the *modus operandi*, type of radicalized domestic terrorist, and type of target had all been expected, which was why the emergency services were so well prepared. The idea of an all-source all-agency analysis body has been borne out, and is being copied internationally.

David Omand also took over the Cabinet secretary's function in relation to agency funding:

I developed the ability of the community as a whole to look at strategic issues and therefore at future funding needs, and had, for example in 2003, put the case for an immediate increase in the size of the Security Service, with corresponding increases in the other two agencies and the police, which the PM and chancellor had accepted.

Likewise, outside the intelligence budget, he had been able to look across Whitehall departments at the future developing of spending on protection and preparation for civil contingencies, and at connecting this to the needs of taking a strategic view of resilience. This was rebuilding a national capacity to recover from disasters that had been run down at the end of the Cold War.

He concluded:

In some ways, the rethinking needed was comparable to that required in the early days of the Cold War, although for very different reasons and this time without the secrecy of those days.

Asked whether his changes were now a fixed part of the system, he replied in the affirmative, though with a caveat familiar to any civil servant:

Yes, at least for the next 10 years, but no part of government should be regarded as immune from development if needs change.

For his part, Butler saw the need for a further central appointment:

> The Cabinet Office used to have high-powered, though part-time scientific advice available, for example through Lord Cherwell, Lord Zuckerman and Dr Frank Panton…individuals could, when necessary, challenge conventional wisdom.
> We conclude that it may be worth considering the appointment of a distinguished scientist to undertake a part-time role as adviser to the Cabinet Office.[51]

Finally, Butler proposed that thought should be given to the fact that the creation of the post of Security and Intelligence Co-ordinator had split the responsibilities of the Cabinet secretary, with the effect that

> …the Cabinet Secretary is no longer so directly involved in *the chain through which intelligence reaches the Prime Minister*. It follows that the Cabinet Secretary, who attends the Cabinet and maintains the machinery to support their decision-making, is less directly involved personally in advising the Prime Minister on security and intelligence issues. By the same token, the Security and Intelligence Co-ordinator does not attend Cabinet and is not part of the Cabinet Secretariat supporting Cabinet Ministers in discharging their collective responsibilities in defence and overseas policy matters.[52] [our emphasis]

As we have seen, the appointment of Richard Mottram as both Co-ordinator and JIC chairman means that, in future, the prime minister will have a single advisor on substantive intelligence and intelligence management issues. But it is unclear whether Mottram, like the Cabinet secretary, will attend Cabinet meetings and be able to advise the Cabinet collectively on intelligence issues. If he does not, Butler's implicit criticism remains; if he does, this will be yet another task for a very busy man.

Moving to the wider field of the management of the UK intelligence machine, it must be said that it has never been very clear what 'coordination' is meant to involve, and how much power the Security and Intelligence Co-ordinator has or should have. Prior to Mottram's appointment, Bill Jeffrey was said to have duties to 'prevent and/or prepare for a major terrorist attack on Britain', in addition to his 'coordination' role.[53] As Accounting Officer for the Single Intelligence Account (SIA – formerly the Single Intelligence Vote

(SIV)) – the pot of money out of which the three Agencies' budgets are paid – the Co-ordinator has had considerable potential to shape the development of UK intelligence, and could, therefore, be seen as 'first among equals'. But the Agencies have always resisted the sort of centralization that could limit their autonomy; the concept of a UK 'director of central intelligence' similar to that in the US (and even more so of a 'director of national intelligence') is anathema to them.

The ISC's 2004–05 report outlines the ways in which the process of coordination had been developed over the previous twelve months (and against the backdrop of the WMD fiasco). In 2002, the rationale for the Co-ordinator post had been spelled out by David Omand and Sir Andrew Turnbull, the then Cabinet secretary:

> They stressed that the main reason for the creation of the position was to have an individual in place who could devote significant time to security, intelligence and resilience matters in an evolving threat environment.[54]

In September 2004, the ISC went back to Sir Andrew, who noted that, in addition to an overarching duty to ensure the good conduct of government and that the 'proper advice' reached the prime minister, the Cabinet secretary had historically had responsibilities for security and intelligence. He was, however, by no means a 'direct source of advice' in this area (nor, as he stressed, in foreign affairs, on the economy and so forth) so that it seemed sensible, in the changed environment after 9/11, to let someone with what was, in effect, greater expertise assume this part of his duties.

This appears eminently sensible, but one must pause and ask what really changed after 9/11. 'Homeland security' had long been a concern, all be it not specifically identified as such, while the issues involved in the strategic management of the UK intelligence community had not changed fundamentally since 2001. What had changed, however, was the public attention devoted to UK intelligence, after a decade in which it had suffered not-so-benign neglect as the 'peace dividend' was cashed in. It could be argued that the new Security and Intelligence Co-ordinator position, with all its current responsibilities, was one that should have been established long before. But it was not, and we need to return to the question of intelligence advice to the prime minister as it has developed in recent years.

David Omand bore his duties lightly and, in the eyes of the

ISC, fulfilled his role well. His part in the construction of JTAC (the Joint Terrorism Analysis Centre) – which has achieved almost iconic status among intelligence experts – was seen as an example of his skill. However, in listing the duties of the post, the ISC seemed to some observers implicitly to question the ability of a single individual to execute so many tasks. If this is a real concern, then it must be even more so for Mottram, who, if he assumes all his predecessor's responsibilities, will not only chair the JIC, but act as Accounting Officer for the Single Intelligence Account, chair the Permanent Secretaries' Committee on the Intelligence Services (PSIS), chair the central Official Committee to ensure delivery of CONTEST (the UK's five-year counter-terrorism strategy), chair the US/UK Joint Contact Group on Homeland Security, the Official Committee on Security (SO), and deliver 'oversight' of the Civil Contingencies Secretariat and the Intelligence and Security Secretariat, which includes the Assessments Staff. If he continues to follow his predecessor, Mottram will also be required to provide 'support' to the CSI – the only government committee with an overview of the Agencies and the rest of the intelligence community, and the one which the prime minister has appeared so reluctant to chair. Finally, as if all this were not enough, '…in the event of any serious incident requiring central government coordination [the Co-ordinator] acts as the government's senior Crisis Manager'.[55]

Mottram's appointment as both chairman of the JIC and Security and Intelligence Co-ordinator is not just a return to the situation that pertained from 1998 to 2002, when the positions of chairman JIC and (old-style) Intelligence Co-ordinator were combined, since before David Omand the Co-ordinator's role was more limited and his status lower. Now the exceptional span of Mottram's apparent responsibilities raises some interesting questions about the central management of the UK intelligence community:

- How will he divide his time between the day-to-day chairmanship of the JIC, his personal intelligence advice to the prime minister, and coordination and top-level management of the UK intelligence community?
- In an intelligence-related crisis requiring nearly full-time concentration on external developments, assessments and briefings to the prime minister and the COBRA crisis group,[56] who minds the management shop?

- In a security crisis, such as a major terrorist attack requiring Mottram to act as 'the government's senior Crisis Manager', who minds the assessment shop and provides intelligence advice to the prime minister and ministers?[57]
- Is Mottram going to require a senior deputy who can take the strain when required?
- What sort of support machinery will the combined post require – is a combined central secretariat for both assessment and community management the answer?
- Is this the beginning of a much-strengthened central intelligence focus for the UK intelligence community, with a concomitant decline in the power of the individual agencies?

As both the Cabinet Office and the fourth ISC have still to pronounce on such issues, one can only speculate. But the creation of the new position moves the UK intelligence community into a new phase, and the ISC will surely want to monitor developments closely.

THE ROLE OF MINISTERS

Like Lord Butler, the ISC formed the view that the issue of advice to the prime minister was, first and foremost, one of *process*, but also significantly one of *personality*; that within the procedural system, the need was for good 'coordination' rather than commonsense, reality-tested advice, and, in terms of personnel, seniority was what was key. For its 1999–2000 report, the ISC

> …took evidence on the process of establishing the Agencies' requirements and priorities, in particular the roles of the Ministerial Committee on the Intelligence Services (CSI), the Permanent Secretaries' Committee on the Intelligence Services (PSIS) and the Joint Intelligence Committee (JIC).[58]

In its pursuit of the facts, the ISC investigated the role of ministers, the JIC, the Security and Intelligence Co-ordinator and the Agencies' customers in establishing, authorizing and verifying the national intelligence requirements (the requirements and priorities for secret intelligence for SIS and GCHQ). The ISC stressed that the national intelligence requirements paper was a very important document: it took a five-year forward look, but with particular concentration on the year ahead.

A distinction was properly drawn between the Security Service and the other secret Agencies in respect of the Requirements paper because the Security Service's priorities were directly determined by its own statutory functions. These included the duty to protect the UK against substantial, covertly organized threats, primarily from terrorism, espionage and the proliferation of weapons of mass destruction, and to support law enforcement agencies in fighting serious crime. However, while needing to react rapidly to changes in these threats, the Security Service paid attention to the national intelligence requirements in drawing up its own priorities. The Security Service's work was also reviewed and validated by a separate Cabinet Office committee, known as the Sub-Committee on Security Service Priorities and Performance, and then agreed by ministers.

In this process, the 1999–2000 annual report noted that an especially important role was played by the *then* Intelligence Co-ordinator (not to be confused with the *later* and more senior Security and Intelligence Co-ordinator post created in 2002 and first filled by David Omand, whose views on the earlier post we have already recorded). An important part of the (old-style) Intelligence Co-ordinator's job was to compile the national intelligence requirements paper, following a series of discussions with the customers of secret intelligence within Whitehall and other organizations, such as the police and the Agencies. The paper was then endorsed by the JIC before being passed to the Permanent Secretaries' Committee on the Intelligence Services, chaired by the Cabinet secretary. PSIS was also required to consider the Agencies' budgets, endorse the national intelligence requirements, and then pass them on to ministers for formal approval.

One might have expected the national intelligence requirements to have been considered by the most senior government body with responsibility for intelligence matters, the Ministerial Committee on the Intelligence Services, chaired by the prime minister. However, to the obvious disgust of the ISC, it emerged from its questions that the CSI had not, in fact, met since 1995 – and that the Permanent Secretaries' Committee on the Intelligence Services had met only three times since 1997. Not surprisingly in the circumstances, the ISC repeatedly said that the Ministerial Committee should meet at least once a year, if only to approve the national intelligence requirements and the Agencies' budgets.

The ISC believed the Blair style of government had highlighted other deficiencies as well. As has been noted, the decision was taken in 1998 to combine the position of JIC chair with that of the (old-style) Intelligence Co-ordinator. The aim was to permit the 'central Government customer', the JIC chair, to set the Agencies' requirements and advise on their funding needs. However, in the view of the ISC, this could lead to a situation in which the JIC chairman/Intelligence Co-ordinator was someone without any agency experience (they no doubt had someone from the FCO in mind – the FCO traditionally provided the JIC chairman), which would have the effect of reducing the post in 'influence and scale'. Furthermore, the ISC argued that the position of Co-ordinator was not sufficiently senior in Whitehall terms to have much impact on governance at the highest levels. In 2000, therefore, the ISC was warning that the combined JIC chairman/Intelligence Co-ordinator might not have

> ...sufficient authority and influence to formulate and implement policy, as well as offer guidance to the Agencies.[59]

The obvious implication was that this would either lead to a serious hole in the centre of intelligence governance in the UK (as evidenced by 'a void at the centre', as the ISC put it, in the context of intelligence community IT[60]) or give a prime minister – *the* prime minister – overarching power in constructing intelligence policy and intelligence-led policy. This mirrors the concerns expressed by Lord Butler *four years later*:

> We see a strong case for the post of Chairman of the JIC being held by someone with experience of dealing with Ministers in a very senior role, and who is demonstrably beyond influence, and thus probably in his last post.[61]

The government's refusal to deal with this matter at an earlier stage had more than a little to do with its subsequent failures over the September 2002 dossier and the WMD fiasco. However, the ISC's original recommendations did not cut any ice with the government, either in 2000 or when the issue was revisited by the third Committee, in its 2001–02 report:

> The Committee notes that CSI has still not formally met to endorse the UK's Requirements and Priorities for Secret Intelligence or the SIA, despite the strong recommendation of the previous Committee that it meet at least annually to so do. We questioned a number of CSI members on whether or not they believed that CSI should meet. They believed that it was a matter for CSI Chairman – the Prime Minister. However, they did not express any reasons why CSI should not meet.

> We believe that CSI would provide Ministers with the forum to discuss intelligence-related matters, such as requirements, priorities and funding. The Secretaries of State believe that while they do have to rely heavily on the judgement of those involved in the UK's Requirements and Priorities process, they do discuss priorities and the allocation of effort with the Agencies' heads.[62]

The insouciant belief of the secretaries of state that one-on-one meetings with agency heads were a substitute for what the ISC thought was necessary – a properly constituted ministerial committee chaired by the prime minister – found an echo in the serious concerns expressed by Lord Butler in his report about the ad hoc way in which major foreign policy decisions were being taken by the Blair government. He wrote:

> We received evidence from two former Cabinet Ministers, one of the present and one of a previous administration, who expressed their concern about the informal nature of much of the Government's decision-making process, and the relative lack of use of established Cabinet Committee machinery.[63]

Butler concluded:

> …one inescapable consequence of this was to limit wider collective discussion and consideration by the Cabinet to the frequent but unscripted occasions when the Prime Minister, Foreign Secretary and Defence Secretary briefed the Cabinet orally. Excellent quality papers were written by officials but were not discussed in Cabinet or Cabinet Committee.[64]

In a clear rebuke, Butler attacked the

> …informality and circumscribed character of the Government's procedures which…risks reducing the scope for informed collective political judgement.[65]

MANAGING THE WORK OF THE AGENCIES

The starting point of the context in which the ISC chose to locate its account of the actual business of the Agencies and its scrutiny was the collapse of Communism in Europe. Prior to 1991, the existence of what was perceived as a very real threat to the Western – and British – way of life by the Soviets seemed to the ISC to justify the existence and expenditure of Britain's secret services. As Tom King wrote in the foreword to the 1997–98 annual report, which can be seen to mark a critical point in the Committee's development and maturity of approach,

> [f]or more than 40 years the UK and its NATO allies endured the threatening environment of the Cold War. The genuine menace of an aggressive world power, seeking to subvert and dominate Europe and the wider world, gave abundant justification for substantial defence, intelligence and security structures. In this climate, the case for foreign intelligence and internal security was generally accepted.[66]

This may have been true in general terms, but in practice it had never been an entirely easy thing to achieve: if things went right for the Agencies, it was hard to see why they were needed; but when they went wrong, it was easy to question their competence and usefulness. Even so, public ignorance was widespread and not necessarily a good thing. As Tom King explained:

> It has been said that the public view of intelligence owes more to fiction than to fact. In the UK with the popularity of Fleming and le Carré there has been no shortage of fiction, but there has been a steady supply of facts as well, with a sequence of notorious defections and spy scandals. These raised many suspicions that all was far from well in our intelligence and security services. At the same time, they served to reinforce in the public mind that the country was under threat, and that we needed those same services to protect us.[67]

Once Soviet power had appeared to collapse, that consent could no longer be taken for granted, and it also raised the question of what our secret Agencies should be required to deliver in the future. The ISC pointed out that

> [t]he dust had barely settled from the sudden fall of the Berlin Wall, and the collapse of the Soviet Union and the Warsaw pact, before Iraq's invasion of Kuwait and the collapse of Yugoslavia created new situations of profound concern for us, and new challenges for intelligence.[68]

The 1997–98 annual report proceeded to describe the growth in organized crime, funded significantly by the worldwide trade in drugs:

> The collapse of the Soviet Union and the removal of barriers to travel from those countries let loose dangerous new criminal

groups, often including ex-members of the KGB and other intelligence and security services. They have a substantial involvement in drugs and money laundering and, increasingly, in the traffic in illegal immigrants which is now a major concern in all European countries.[69]

In addition to international crime, the ISC noted (in 1998) that 'the risk of proliferation of WMD has long been recognised as a serious threat' and it also outlined the dangers of terrorism:

> In recent years terrorist attacks of all kinds world-wide have averaged almost 60 per month. In the UK we have all too long an experience of terrorism. Elsewhere there is increasing concern over the Islamic terrorist threat...Whilst we may not have been so affected ourselves by these groups, some of them have used Britain as their base to raise funds and equipment and recruit new members.[70]

In its 1997–98 report, the ISC specified a number of areas in which changed requirements were being levied on the secret Agencies, or in which, in the case of the Security Service, it had decided it needed to act.

It highlighted as an important change the 'raising of the priority of work against drugs trafficking to the First Order of importance', which involved SIS and GCHQ, as well as the Security Service. C/SIS had told the ISC it was 'going up the supply chain', developing 'major projects against suppliers' and the director of GCHQ reported 'a significant rise in the number of requests by the law enforcement agencies to take action on sigint [signals intelligence] reports on these subjects'.

Northern Ireland, on the other hand, had seen renewed ceasefires, with a consequent five per cent decline in expenditure on intelligence operations there, although this was counterbalanced by increased work against international terrorism and WMD proliferation, espionage and organized crime. The duties of the Security Service in respect of its 'lead advisory role to Government on protective security' now included a 'Penetration Risk Assessment Group'. Its purpose was to provide 'fresh impetus' to countering the 'continuing risks of penetration by foreign intelligence services' but also 'the risks associated with staff exposure to corruption and intimidation by criminals in the course of the Service's new work against serious organised crime'.

These tasks imply that two important developments were under way. The first was that the collapse of the Soviet Union had by no means ended the threat of foreign intelligence penetration (and, possibly, that behind-the-scenes evidence of penetration prior to 1991 was coming to light – as shown by the revelations from the Mitrokhin archives, discussed later). Second, however, it would seem that intelligence officers had been confronted with offers of cash and other favours, not to mention threats, while seeking to operate against serious organized criminals. This, too, was a matter about which there was little, if any, public knowledge prior to this report, and was an issue to be taken seriously. Whereas revelations about communist espionage (which had not been known about at the time it took place) implied at least some Security Service lapses (or at least unconcern about past misdemeanours), bribes and threats to intelligence officers working on international crime in the late 1990s indicated that some of their targets might know they were under operational investigation. Were this the case, it would be a dangerous development, not least because it would show that the Agencies' secret work might have been less secret in this area than was imagined.

THE SECURITY SERVICE'S FILES

The final major concern the ISC highlighted in 1997–98 (and which continued to exercise the Committee in subsequent years) had to do with a genuine civil liberties problem – the creation, use and destruction of personal files, in particular those involving British citizens. It is a truism that the strength of any security service depends on the extent and reliability of its files, and the ISC was right to acknowledge that 'Security Service files are at the heart of much of the Service's work'.[71] At the same time, the existence of such files had caused successive governments considerable problems, and the line taken by the ISC was somewhat ambiguous. It is evidence that the ISC was itself divided on whether to regard the Security Service's file-keeping work as in, or against, the interests of parliamentary democracy.

On the one hand, it was clear to it that sound and extensive files were a key, arguably *the* key, Security Service asset. On the other hand, the ISC felt the possession of large numbers of sensitive files laid the Security Service open to the charge that it was behaving like a secret police. As the ISC itself noted,

> [t]hey [the Security Service files] are the subject of a significant proportion of the complaints to the Security Service Tribunal; of continuing debate in Parliament and, last year, of allegations in the national press by an ex-member of the Service.[72]

Similarly, while the ISC demanded assurances that sensitive information about individuals was 'afforded a sufficient degree of protection' and that individuals might have some unspecified opportunity to 'protect' themselves against 'information inappropriately or inaccurately stored and used against their interests', it was also (and naturally) concerned that the Security Service would not resort to the simple expedient of destroying such files.[73]

Surprisingly, however, the reason the ISC gave for its concern was *not* that files should be preserved because they provided information on individuals who might well merit attention, even if doing so caused political problems. Rather, the ISC said it was worried about the need for

> ...safeguards against any possibility that the Security Service could use its control of the retention or destruction of files to *rewrite the historical record*.[74] [our emphasis]

This suggestion is a revealing indicator of the ISC's perception of itself as a bridge between the Agencies and the public. The very thought that the Security Service might be minded to 'rewrite the historical record' was shocking enough, but to imply that it was a real possibility was even more disturbing.

It could, however, be argued that the truly dangerous outcome of such concerns was not just that the Security Service might think twice about opening files on potentially dangerous political targets because one day they might be in a position to make a fuss about it, but that it might decide that a policy of mass file destruction was the safest way of ensuring that the issue would not flare up in the future. Far from underwriting the Security Service's work, and sustaining it against political pressure, the ISC appeared to be encouraging the public to be sceptical about the Security Service, pushing the Security Service in the direction of choosing not to know things, rather than bolstering the idea that the more it understands about the enemies of democracy, the more useful its work becomes.

Indeed, the ISC went on to examine in some detail the Security Service's policy on file destruction, seemingly adopting, as its point of departure, the notion – which could be viewed as either pragmatic or bizarre – that destroying files was probably wiser than retaining them. At the same time, the ISC expressed what might seem a contradictory caveat – evidence, perhaps, that it was itself more than a little divided on this critical question – noting that, prior to 1970, the Security Service had 'weeded and destroyed' its files but that 'this policy was found to have seriously hampered the investigation of a number of espionage cases'. It was, of course, in the 1970s that Venona decrypts and defector evidence began to illuminate the extent of the KGB's and GRU's penetration of UK government institutions, leading to the unmasking of Sir Anthony Blunt and John Cairncross, and the difficult investigations of Sir Roger Hollis, a former director general of the Security Service. Not surprisingly, the Security Service decided that, in future, files would be microfiched rather than destroyed.

What was certainly remarkable, however, was that, on the apparent collapse of Communism in 1992, the Security Service changed tack again and

> …reconsidered its files policy again in the light of the changing nature of the threat with the end of the Cold War, and the decline in the threat from subversion, i.e. actions intended to overthrow or undermine parliamentary democracy by political, industrial or violent means.[75]

The ISC listed the duties of the various Agencies. The Security Service's role was simply to 'protect national security, safeguard economic well-being and support the prevention and detection of serious crime'.[76] While the phrase 'the decline in the threat from subversion' implies that some degree of subversion still existed, the Security Service had evidently concluded that this was not something that required any positive action on its part:

> …110,000 files have been destroyed or 'marked for destruction' so far. The vast majority of these relate to *subversion, on which the Service is no longer conducting any investigations.*[77] [our emphasis]

This admission, tucked away in paragraph 47 of the 1997–98 report, represents something of a bombshell, and it appears that the ISC was – quite properly – not entirely happy that it represented best practice in the world of security. For one thing, it could be read as suggesting that a *political* decision had been taken that 'subversive' actions and attitudes that had been deemed, with some justification, for very many years to constitute threats to liberal democracy in Britain were, at a stroke, to be discounted. It could also suggest that a *political* decision had been taken, either by the Security Service or the government, that there were to be no further historically inspired or motivated investigations of individuals (a decision that would, in due course, backfire on the Security Service when the Mitrokhin material became public).

Finally, and perhaps most controversially, it ignored two important factors in helping to keep Britain secure in a post-communist environment. The first was the possibility that individuals who had been officers of one kind or another in the former communist secret services, and involved in subversive activities, could have transferred their allegiances and skills to other revolutionary or anti-democratic and anti-Western regimes. For this reason, the names and identities of such people should not have been destroyed, even if the regimes for which they worked no longer existed. Secondly, individual Britons who might have acted as the agents of these officers in the 1980s could, in the same way, transfer their allegiance to other left-wing or extremist causes in the 1990s and beyond.

We know today that those who worked from within the UK to support the aims and ambitions of Communism were motivated to act not just by intellectual arguments, but also because they were subject to peer group encouragement and because they possessed certain personal characteristics (they were often, for example, good risk takers). The destruction of files for *political* reasons would make no security sense whatsoever, either in detecting the activities of 'officers' and agent runners, or in uncovering their agents. In the event, as has already been noted, the Security Service destroyed 110,000 files – almost fifty per cent of its 1997 holdings – after 1992. However, subversion may continue to exist whether or not it is investigated, and a policy made (in this case, not to investigate subversion) can easily be unmade. Once a file is destroyed, however, that whole investment in security is made nugatory.[78]

The ISC's obvious unease at this policy of destruction could be seen in its suggestion that 'some form of independent check should be built into the process *particularly in respect of files relating to subversion*'[79] (our emphasis), while it noted that 'ultimately, the judgement in respect of the review and destruction of individual files is made solely by the Security Service'. Given the inherent contradiction between external review and Security Service autonomy, it is not surprising that the government rejected the Committee's suggestion that there should be an external check on file destruction.[80]

In fairness, the Security Service could argue that it was merely following the logic of its own definitions, and that its cessation of work on 'subversion' did not mean that it was blind to associated threats. These would include espionage and terrorism aimed against the UK but not specifically 'intended to overthrow or undermine parliamentary democracy' – rather (for espionage) to obtain our secrets or (for terrorism) to coerce the government into changing its policies. The Security Service would also, no doubt, indignantly reject any suggestion that its policy on the destruction of files was the result of any *political* decision, and might be expected to maintain that it reflected a *policy* decision (which could have been a directive from the home secretary, the results of an internal Security Service review, or the result of consultation between both parties). But this argument is not one that is aired in the Committee's report.

The ISC pointed to the different policy towards files adopted by SIS. Here files on individuals were held chiefly if they related to agency staff, agents, former agents, and others with whom SIS had contact. It possessed 86,000 such records, some dating back to 1909. What was more, SIS retained most of its files for both historical and operational reasons, accepting, unlike the Security Service, that there was an 'operational value of reference back to files, sometimes after many years'.[81] GCHQ's policy on files was entirely different, again for operational reasons.

As if to balance what seems to be a very justified scepticism towards the Security Service's files policy, the ISC made a final observation on the broader issue of files in its 1997–98 annual report. It was a fret over the use of Security Service information by an incoming prime minister in relation to the formation of a government. The ISC noted that a new prime minister would be given 'relevant national security information concerning for example contacts with a foreign intelligence service' held on candidates for election (the ISC does not consider whether such information might be made available in the case of peers who might be asked to join the government). It also disclosed that a similar service had been provided to the leader of the opposition since 1992.

However, the ISC sounded a note of real warning to the Security Service about this. It emphasized:

> There is a heavy responsibility on the Director-General, in putting forward any such file, to ensure the information on it has been properly checked and relates solely to national security.[82]

The ISC was plainly aware of the potential damage that false accusations could cause an aspiring appointee to the Cabinet. Yet it failed to add that the disappearance of genuinely incriminating information concerning a prospective appointee because of the policy of file destruction would be every bit as damaging as a false accusation (and arguably more so), especially in respect of any contact an individual might have had to a foreign intelligence service.

An analogous, but perhaps rather more bizarre, accompaniment to this issue was the question, raised in the 2001–02 report, about the tapping of the telephones of members of either House of Parliament.[83] It had arisen in response to a question to the prime minister. Tony Blair had replied that the position of his government was as outlined by his predecessor, Harold Wilson, who had 'given instructions that there was to be no tapping of the telephones of Members of the House of Commons [sic]', adding that, if he was obliged to change this policy, he would announce the fact to Parliament. On 27 December 2000 this policy had been extended to members of the Lords (the government had plainly picked up what seemed to be an anomaly in its policy on tapping). The ISC made it clear that it entirely supported Blair's position, adding that it was 'important it was not eroded in any way'. Wilson's words could, however, be interpreted to mean that *at some stage* following a change in this policy, Parliament would be told, but that this might not be until some time – conceivably years – after the event.

THE DUTIES OF THE AGENCIES

The outlining of the Agencies' duties was a matter addressed in 1998–99, with the ISC appearing to have developed a somewhat arbitrary way of deciding which topics to address. The introduction to the Committee's annual report[84] noted that the previous year had been an exceptionally dangerous one, with a range of serious threats and potential threats to Britain's security. These included a large increase in terrorist attacks throughout the world (averaging sixty per week); those on the American embassies in Nairobi and Dar es Salaam had killed over two hundred people and 'confirmed the scale of the threat posed by Usama bin Laden and other Islamic groups'. Both India and Pakistan had successfully tested nuclear weapons, and other 'most unwelcome setbacks' had included Chinese espionage against the USA and 'the intended betrayal on the Internet of possible members of SIS by a disaffected former member'. For this reason, the ISC had decided to look in detail at the Agencies' work in countering the proliferation of WMD, how well Britain's secrets were protected from information warfare attacks and the security of government communications more generally.

From this, the ISC indicated that it wished to adopt a proactive stance in helping to define the duties of the Agencies. It accepted, of course, that the Security Service had a 'separate committee validating its priorities' (that, to a large extent, meant that the Security Service could set its own agenda), but the two collection agencies had their priorities set by the JIC, and endorsed by ministers. The ISC emphasized its wish that 'sufficient guidance' be given on them and stated that it intended to 'revisit in the coming year the challenging process of establishing requirements and priorities'.[85]

The Committee noted that the Agencies' work to counter the proliferation of WMD was first order of importance in the JIC's requirements and priorities:

> The threat to our armed forces deployed overseas from these weapons is very real, and we believe that the Agencies play a vital role in establishing the threat to our service personnel.[86]

But it was, to put it mildly, less than enthused about the Foreign Office's airy and otherworldly attitude to the success of counter-proliferation measures:

> …we were concerned that the evidence from the Foreign Office appears to suggest that sanctions and control regimes are working. We believe that this view is not backed up by the evidence the Agencies have provided…[87]

These were unusually strong words of condemnation from the Committee, which concluded that

> [w]e believe that a more proactive approach could pay dividends. This would require greater effort by the Agencies to track down and stop proliferators.[88]

However, to do so would also require resources, and the ISC demanded the Agencies manage these changes effectively by a 'reprioritization' of their work. But the Committee's belief that intelligence assets should be used proactively to ensure that WMD proliferation was contained through 'reprioritization' seemed to assume that no extra funding would be forthcoming and that, in financial terms, intelligence was a zero-sum game – something that was true at the time, but changed remarkably after 9/11.

THE RELATIONSHIP BETWEEN THE AGENCIES AND THE MEDIA

As we have seen, the ISC believed it was self-evident that *it* was the authoritative point of contact between the public generally and Britain's secret Agencies. However, it was fully aware that other channels of communication existed between the Agencies – the Security Service and SIS in particular – and the media and political classes. In its 2004–05 annual report, the ISC noted that some journalists had privileged access to the Agencies – in the *patois* of the civil service, they were 'trusties'. There were, as might be expected, numerous problems with the system that had evolved. Some of these problems had to do with the need to try to ensure that what the media gained from the Agencies was accurate and did not jeopardize security interests, while at the same time seeking to prevent the Agencies, should they be so minded, from attempting to influence public opinion, either for their own purposes, or on behalf of a government policy or line.

But although the 2004–05 annual report represented the ISC's first overall look at the relationship between the Agencies and the media, it was not the first time it had been required to address the subject. In 2000, the ISC was asked by then Home Secretary Jack Straw to undertake a full investigation of the implications of an episode involving an attempt by one agency, SIS, to influence public opinion – the 'Mitrokhin Affair'. What SIS wished to achieve was not *political*, which would, of course, have been unconstitutional, and even anti-constitutional, but was more about trying to burnish its image in the public mind.

The background to this extraordinary episode was the appearance at the British Embassy in a 'Baltic State' of Vasili Mitrokhin, the chief archivist of the KGB. He had with him several volumes of notes he had made on the files to which he had access, covering the period from 1917 to 1984. Mitrokhin had, in fact, previously approached the US Embassy in the same country with the same material – only to be told unceremoniously to make himself scarce. Scenting that Mitrokhin's material, if genuine, might prove one of its biggest ever coups, the SIS officer in the Embassy told him to go back and collect more material, and then present himself again that June.

Mitrokhin's material was sent back to the UK and translated, a process begun in 1992 and still continuing in 2000. His motive for sharing his secrets with Britain was, in large part, to 'inflict as much damage as possible to the old KGB and party nomenklatura' by publishing his material. For its part, SIS saw an opportunity to portray itself to the public in a flattering light. For once, perhaps, the public might be persuaded to associate the SIS with a dazzling success, rather than its having to suffer from the more usual and depressing media accusations of deceit and failure.

There were, however, serious practical and theoretical objections to such a course. Publication might hinder the prosecution of any former KGB agents deemed to deserve this, while some former KGB agents might now be working for its successor, the FSB. While the appearance of Mitrokhin's material would teach the public a valuable lesson, namely that Soviet-style secret practices were more alive than many believed, it would also, and obviously, point to the existence of past and perhaps present Russian agents in the UK. This, in turn, would inevitably raise the obvious question as to why SIS's sister agency, the Security Service, had failed to spot this important fact, and why it had failed to bring prosecutions against such people.

SIS's thirst for a PR coup plainly outweighed any more reflective analysis of the dangers that publication would inevitably bring. As a result, in 1995 SIS decided to ask Professor Christopher Andrew of Cambridge University to cooperate with Mitrokhin. In March 1996, the idea was put to then Foreign Secretary Malcolm Rifkind, who agreed it should proceed.

As readers of the book that Andrew and Mitrokhin produced three years later will see, the SIS believed it had very cleverly bypassed the problems stemming from publication by ensuring that any 'live' material was excluded (indeed, careful reading of the book shows that many of the allegations it contains are, quite properly, sourced to already published books and hardly count as 'revelations'). The impact of the work comes from its first chapter, which explains who Mitrokhin was and how his story had come to be told – which was, of course, a newsworthy revelation and doubtless helped sell many copies. It is not clear whether anyone realized that Mitrokhin's revelations would raise questions as to why the individuals of historical interest that he had named had not been prosecuted in the courts at the time, or identified earlier by the Security Service.

We need not review the whole sorry saga here; suffice it to say that the book's attempt to disguise the two main 'historical' spies, John Symonds and Mrs Melita Norwood by using their code names 'Hola' and 'Scot' failed almost immediately, with their identities being revealed in *The Times*. Within two days of the *Times* story appearing, Jack Straw, after consulting the prime minister, invited the Intelligence and Security Committee to conduct an inquiry into the way in which the publication of the Mitrokhin material had been handled.

This was the first time a government minister had called on the ISC to undertake an inquiry of any sort, and marked a key stage in the Committee's development. Previously, the government's reaction would probably have been (after some foot-dragging) to ask one of 'the great and the good' to undertake a one-off inquiry. Now, the government was making use of the ISC as an integral element of the UK's review system. In theory, the Security Commission could have undertaken the task, but the political elements of the case probably ruled out that option.

In responding (and in the larger context this is much more significant), Tom King stipulated that the government should let the ISC see the papers of former administrations and advice to ministers, failing which, he said, the ISC would not investigate. It was the government's agreement to do so that gave the ISC greater powers than any select committee; the importance of this element of the Mitrokhin Affair is often overlooked, but it cannot be overstated.

The ISC's report on the Mitrokhin Affair concluded with a stern rebuke to the Security Service ('serious failure' is about as bad as it gets in official language):

> The Committee believes that it was a serious failure of the Security Service not to refer Mrs Norwood's case to the Law Officers in mid 1993. This failure resulted in the decision not to prosecute Mrs Norwood effectively being taken by the Security Service. The Committee is concerned that the Service used public interest reasons to justify taking no further action against Mrs Norwood, when this was for the Law Officers to decide. We also believe that the failure of the Security Service to interview Mrs Norwood at this time prevented her possible prosecution.
>
> The Committee is concerned that Mrs Norwood's case 'slipped out of sight' between 1993 and 1998. The Committee

believes that Mrs Norwood's case should have been kept under review during this period. This was a further serious failure by the Security Service.[89]

SIS, by contrast, emerged from the whole business smelling of roses, with the ISC handing out a whole bouquet to the Service:

> Carrying the initial contact with Mr Mitrokhin right through to his and his family's successful exfiltration together with all his material represents a major achievement by the SIS. In addition the management of the material and its dissemination, as appropriate, to foreign liaison services was well handled. The Committee wish to pay tribute to this outstanding piece of intelligence work.[90]

Thus SIS's attempt to use the media to its own advantage had succeeded, but at the questionable cost of dropping its sister agency deep in the mire.

THE LATEST SPECIAL REPORTS

It has not been possible here to do more than highlight those themes in the ISC's ten years of report writing that make a wider contribution to our understanding of the ways in which the ISC operates and the subjects of perennial concern to it. However, in addition to its special report on Iraqi WMD, the third ISC produced two further 'one-off' reports on subjects of its own choosing.

The first of these was the December 2002 report *Inquiry into Intelligence, Assessments and Advice prior to the Terrorist Bombings on Bali 12 October 2002*;[91] the second was the March 2005 report on the *Handling of Detainees by UK Intelligence Personnel in Afghanistan and Guantanamo Bay and Iraq*.[92] The former, which we have already touched upon, was thought by Ann Taylor to have been particularly important, and she bracketed it together with the WMD report as 'the most significant of all the reports we wrote'.

For the latter, the ISC took evidence on whether or not 'UK intelligence personnel were involved in, or witnessed any abuses or behaviour contrary to the international conventions or UK policy' and, if so, 'whether any action was taken, whether UK intelligence personnel were sufficiently well trained before they came into contact with detainees', and when ministers were informed there might be problems on this score.

The ISC discovered that UK intelligence personnel conducted or witnessed some 2,000 interviews, and that there were fifteen occasions when they reported 'actual or potential breaches of UK policy or international conventions'. While the ISC accepted that 'it was difficult to balance the duty to obtain intelligence which proved to be valuable and the need to abide by the UK's interpretation of international conventions and to adhere to UK policy', it did make some fairly forthright suggestions to the SIS in particular.

It was said, for example, that SIS and Security Service personnel deployed to Afghanistan and Guantanamo Bay 'were not sufficiently trained in the Geneva Conventions nor were they aware which interrogation techniques the UK had specifically banned in 1972'. It noted that, in January 2002, an SIS officer had reported observations of breaches in interrogation policy 'correctly', and that SIS had responded with instructions that it shared with the Security Service. However, 'these were not definitive enough' and did not spell out that incidents of this nature should have been reported not merely to the senior American officer present, but also to SIS and Security Service headquarters in London, and thence to ministers in the government. The ISC also insisted that, prior to deployment, 'UK intelligence personnel are clearly instructed as to their duties and responsibilities in respect of the treatment of detainees', and that the 'UK should seek agreement with its allies on the methods and standards for the detention, interviewing or interrogation of people detained in these operations'.[93]

HAS THE ISC DELIVERED THE GOODS?

There are many types and flavours of intelligence and security oversight in contemporary political systems worldwide. This book concentrates on the UK's unique solution to oversight, comparing it mainly with the systems of the United States and Canada, but with some reference to those of Australia and New Zealand. We have done so because, like the other members of the post-war '5-Eyes Community',[94] in the twentieth century we were not defeated by our enemies in war, whether 'hot' or 'cold'; we experienced no seizure of power by any totalitarian movement; and our intelligence and security organizations were not seen as instruments of a repressive regime that needed to be tamed. In short, our perceptions of how we need intelligence and security services to operate, and how they should be regulated and overseen, have been very different from many of our European partners with more troubled pasts.[95] Possibly for straightforward reasons of a common political heritage and language, but also because of the sheer scale of the global superpower's intelligence activities and domestic concerns – however misplaced – about intelligence wrongdoing, it has been the US experience of intelligence oversight that has chiefly shaped our thinking on this crucial area of governance.

Whatever the reasons our American allies looked to oversight, and however much the UK public may feel that the purpose of oversight is to keep a stern check on agencies that – potentially – wield much power, *in practice* British oversight today has attempted to expend as much energy on tracking government errors of management as it has on intelligence and security service shortcomings. The question 'has the ISC delivered the goods?' therefore invites another: 'what are the goods the ISC has set out to deliver?'

There can be no simple answer to this question, not least because any book such as this is inevitably written from a position outside the 'ring of secrecy' and can only judge the work of the Committee by its outputs, with no direct access to its internal deliberations over objectives. Moreover, we have reviewed the ISC's work over more than a decade, a period that covers three Committees, two chairs and a total (including the chair) of twenty members. There can be no doubt that the ISC has sought conscientiously to meet its statutory responsibilities and to pursue many associated issues, even if some of these have, at times, appeared to result from personal preoccupations rather than a corporate agenda.

The fourth Committee is now well embarked upon its responsibilities. Unless it were to maintain that its predecessors had reached a state of perfection, it would have to accept that improvements are always possible. Its predecessor's 2002 brochure certainly saw room for improvement:

> The system of oversight exercised by the ISC has evolved since its establishment in 1994 and it will, without doubt, continue to do so. Oversight of the intelligence and security Agencies is now regarded as an important part of democratic society and any future developments will be based on the foundations created by the ISC.[96]

In our final chapter we will suggest a number of ways in which we believe the Committee could exercise its oversight responsibilities more effectively. Some of these are highly practical measures; others raise fundamental questions of responsibility and authority that go to the heart of the ISC's *raison d'être*. But before we reach our conclusions, it is necessary, having looked in this chapter at intelligence oversight as a concept, to see in the next how this concept can and should be applied to the UK, with its delightfully imprecise constitutional framework.

1 *Inquiry into Intelligence, Assessment and Advice prior to the Terrorist Bombings on Bali 12 October 2002*, Cm 5724, December 2002, paras 20–35.
2 'Government Response to the Intelligence and Security Committee Inquiry into Intelligence Assessments and Advice prior to the Terrorist Bombings on Bali 12 October 2002', Cm 5765, February 2003, paras 7, 8, 10.
3 Examples include the 'Ricin' trial and the November 2005 acquittal of Parveen Sharif of failing to tell police about her brother's plan to blow up a Tel Aviv bar in 2003.
4 ISC Annual Report 2004–05, Cm 6510, April 2005, para. 5.
5 Quoted in the *Guardian*, 17 March 2004.
6 Some of the issues that we have ignored, such as postal interception, are comparatively trivial and appear to reflect the concerns of individual ISC members rather than the main stream of its work; others, such as its concern over the cost of relocating GCHQ to its new headquarters, are self-contained and do not contribute to the broad thrust of our arguments.
7 Cm 6510.
8 Interviewed by Jeremy Paxman on *Newsnight*, 16 January 2006.
9 Cm 6510.
10 *Ibid.*, para. 2.
11 *Iraqi Weapons of Mass Destruction – Intelligence and Assessments*, Cm 5972, September 2003.
12 Cm 6510, paras 61–63.
13 *Ibid.*, para 64.
14 Cm 5972.
15 *Hansard*, 4 June 2003, Col. 149, quoted in Cm 5972, para. 14.
16 *Panorama*, 11 July 2004.
17 Cm 5972, paras 32, 66 and 115.
18 Lord Butler of Brockwell, *Review of Intelligence on Weapons of Mass Destruction* (London: TSO, 2004), para. 466 (*Butler Report*).
19 Cm 5972, paras 72,73.
20 *Ibid.*, para 57.
21 Sir Christopher Meyer, *DC Confidential: The Confidential Memoirs of Britain's Ambassador to the US at the Time of 9/11 and the Iraq War* (London: Weidenfeld & Nicolson, 2005), p. 284.
22 *Guardian*, 15 February 2006.

23 In fact, SIS does not assess intelligence; it produces intelligence reports, which others (the JIC, DIS) use in producing their assessments. The Security Service, however, does produce assessments.
24 Cm 6510, Conclusion N.
25 Cm 6510, para. 4.
26 *Ibid.*, para. 4.
27 *Ibid.*, para. 5.
28 To put this figure into proportion (and without wishing to underestimate its significance in both general and personal terms) it represents about 30 deaths a year, or rather less than 1% of the annual death rate on UK roads.
29 Cm 6510, para. 5.
30 *Ibid.*, paras 3–5.
31 *Ibid.*, paras 80–88.
32 The list of those who gave evidence to the ISC was given in the report (not always correctly) as follows: BBC: Ms Helen Boaden (Head of News), Mr Stephen Whittle; *Guardian*: Mr Alan Rushbridger (*sic* – correctly Rusbridger) (Editor), Mr Richard Norton-Taylor; *Daily Telegraph*: Mr Michael Smith; *Financial Times*: Mr Andrew Gowers (Editor); *Mail on Sunday*: Mr Peter Wright (Editor), Mr John Wellington; *Sunday Times*: Mr John Withrow (*sic* – correctly Witherow) (Editor). It should be stressed that these are *not* those reporters regarded as 'trusties' by the Agencies.
33 *Hansard*, 8 July 2004, Col. 1068.
34 Morrison interview on *Today*, 28 October 2004.
35 See Anthony Glees' letter to the *Sunday Times*, 1 August 2004. He wrote 'if the ISC kowtows to political pressure, its point is entirely lost'.
36 Some observers believe that Tom King would have told the Agencies not to interfere in the internal administration of the ISC.
37 *Butler Report*, p. 141.
38 *Ibid.*, p. 142.
39 *Intelligence Oversight*, at www.cabinetoffice.gov.uk/publications/reports/intelligence/intel.pdf
40 *Ibid.*, p. 13.
41 Select Committee on Home Affairs (third report, session 1998–99), *Accountability of the Security Service*, HC 291, 14 June 1999, para 5.
42 *Intelligence Oversight*, p. 14.
43 ISC May 1995 Interim Report, Cm 2873.
44 ISC Annual Report 2001–02, Cm 5542, p. 6.
45 Notably the Interception of Communications Commissioner, the Intelligence Services Commissioner and the Investigatory Powers Tribunal.
46 Cm 2873, Introductory Letter.
47 At one stage during the Iraq crisis Dr John Reid, then Labour Party chairman, said that intelligence officers who were believed to be briefing against the government and undermining its case that Iraq

possessed WMD were 'rogue elements'. See Anthony Glees and Philip Davies, *Spinning the Spies: Intelligence, Open Government and the Hutton Inquiry* (London: Social Affairs Unit, 2004), pp. 58–59.
48 Cm 2873.
49 ISC Annual Report 2003–04, Cm 6240, pp. 31–32.
50 *Butler Report*, p. 144.
51 *Ibid.*, p. 145.
52 *Ibid.*, p. 147. Lord Butler added: 'We understand that the ISC will shortly review how this arrangement has worked.'
53 *The Times*, 5 January 2005.
54 Cm 6510, p. 7.
55 Cabinet Office press release on Jeffrey's appointment, 18 April 2005.
56 Perhaps disappointingly, in view of its menacing acronym, COBRA obtains its name from its venue – Cabinet Office Briefing Room 'A'.
57 In principle, this should not prove a major problem, as the JIC chairman has two deputies: the director general, defence and intelligence in the FCO, and the chief of defence intelligence. However, neither deputy would have been as used to briefing the prime minister and Cabinet ministers as the chairman.
58 ISC Annual Report 1999–2000, Cm 4897, November 2000, p. 7.
59 *Ibid.*, p. 10.
60 *Ibid.*, p. 17.
61 *Butler Report*, p. 144.
62 Cm 5542, para. 10.
63 *Butler Report*, pp. 146–47.
64 *Ibid.*, p. 147.
65 *Ibid.*, p. 148.
66 ISC Annual Report 1997–98, Cm 4073, p. v.
67 *Ibid.*
68 *Ibid.*, p. 6.
69 *Ibid.*
70 *Ibid.*
71 *Ibid.*, p. 16.
72 *Ibid.*
73 *Ibid.*
74 *Ibid.*
75 *Ibid.*, p. 19.
76 These duties were set out in the 1989 and 1996 Security Acts.
77 Cm 4073, p. 19.
78 It is true that the precise meaning of 'subversion' has yet to be agreed. 'Terror' masquerading as 'free speech' is perhaps the best contemporary variant of the much older desire of certain groups to defeat the basic principles of liberal democracy by using them to undermine it.
79 Cm 4073, p. 20.
80 *The Government's Response*, October 1998, Cm 4089.
81 Cm 4073, p. 21.
82 *Ibid.*, p. 19.

83 Cm 5542, p. 17.
84 ISC Annual Report 1998–99, Cm 4532, November 1999, p. v.
85 *Ibid.*, p. 8.
86 *Ibid.*, p. 22.
87 *Ibid.*, p 24.
88 *Ibid.*
89 *The Mitrokhin Inquiry Report*, Cm 4764, June 2000, Conclusions B & C. The Security Service was, however, given at least one lifeline by the ISC. It focused only on the KGB spies 'Hola' and 'Scot'; the revelations about Stasi spies were, significantly, not merely not pursued in this report but doubt was cast on whether 'spy' was the correct word for them. The Committee wrote: 'The BBC series and articles in the press also identified other "spies" [sic] who had never been prosecuted by the UK authorities but had been identified in the records of the former East German Secret Police, the Stasi.' Those double quote marks say it all (though interestingly, tucked away in the report, we find Lander's written comments to the ISC stating that 'pressure of work on other Mitrokhin cases and on Stasi and other leads, resulted in this case [that of "Hola"] slipping out of sight between November 1993 and August 1998'.
90 *Ibid.*, Conclusion A.
91 Cm 5724, December 2002.
92 *Handling of Detainees by UK Intelligence Personnel in Afghanistan and Guantanamo Bay and Iraq*, Cm 6469, March 2005.
93 *Ibid.*, pp. 28–29.
94 New Zealand was formally excluded by the US as a full 'AUSCANNZUKUS' partner in 1985 after it refused to allow a port visit by a nuclear-armed US destroyer – but agency-level contacts continued.
95 In referring to European countries, we are very conscious that the South African experience presents many of the same features as encountered in Eastern Europe in the move from a repressive to a democratic system.
96 *Intelligence Oversight*, p. 12.

CHAPTER 5

THE ISC AND THE ALTERNATIVE RATIONALE FOR OVERSIGHT

In retrospect, we can see that the ISC, for all its strengths and weaknesses, represents a significant contribution to the rationale for, as well as the practice of, intelligence accountability and oversight. Unlike its British and American predecessors in the growing, multinational intelligence oversight community, it was not born as a result of an ill-informed moral panic fostered and manipulated by ideologues and politicians for partisan reasons. It was, instead, a product of a quintessentially British approach to reform built through incrementalism – the ISC was one of a series of legislative initiatives regulating intelligence that began with the 1985 Interception of Communications Act (IOCA) and continued *after* ISA 1994 to include the 2000 Regulation of Investigatory Powers Act (RIPA)[1] – and compromise, stabilized by sober second thought. While one might point to the Scott inquiry having a propelling role analogous in some ways to the driving role (described in Chapter 3) of Church and Pike in America or MacDonald in Canada, the British inquiry was more about intelligence–government coordination than any putative intelligence wrongdoing.

Even at their worst, the intelligence agencies in the English-speaking world have presented a less menacing political profile than those in nominal democracies with weaker liberal traditions. As a result, while some of our continental European allies might have need to worry about a security service that blows up policemen[2] or one that quietly murders foreign politicians in country villas,[3] these are not the kind of excesses with which we have ever had to concern ourselves. Indeed, not even the worst excesses of Hoover's FBI approached such extremes. When the Parliamentary Assembly of the Council of Europe opines that 'Since…internal security services are often inadequately controlled, there is a high risk of abuse of power and violations of human rights, unless legislative safeguards are provided',[4] they are speaking more to the continental experience than the British, an experience that is not truly relevant to the UK's political history and that might even take our legislation in inappropriate and deleterious directions. Indeed, it must surely be significant that the countries most prone to intelligence abuses on the European continent have the least developed administrative and political controls on their agencies, and the least desire to develop such controls. And yet the irony remains that European institutions like the European Court of Human Rights so often presume to stand in judgement on British institutions and methods. John Stuart Mill once expressed the concern that democratic institutions could not thrive without a democratic culture to nourish them.[5] In Britain, the political soils will not easily support anything other than democracy.

Because the ISC was not created out of a moral panic,[6] its mandate and powers do not reflect the same consuming fear of intelligence 'rogue elephants'. Instead, its evolution reflects different selection pressures and different priorities. The basic need for something like the ISC has more to do with the progressively expanded parliamentary oversight and eventual control of the instrumentalities of 'the Crown' that can be traced back to the very outset of parliamentary democracy.[7] It developed, in many respects, as one more incremental step beyond the original Thatcher-era parliamentary select committees, but reflecting and embodying compromise between the political rationale that drove the creation of those committees and the necessities of the secret aspects of state that the Thatcher government itself sought (with decreasing success) to insulate from the parliamentary oversight programme set in train. These two processes were given an additional major impetus once the Major government decided to place the Agencies on a statutory footing and the question of the relationship between Parliament and its statutory bodies could no longer be side-stepped.

We have already set out the argument that the basic rationale for accountability and oversight in liberal democracies needs to be fundamentally rethought. In Chapter 3 we put forward the case for an 'alternative rationale' for oversight that rejects the futile hunt for Senator Church's mythical monster in favour of four alternative criteria for oversight:

- a quality-control 'belt and braces' mechanism intended to support, but not supplant, administrative mechanisms of control and constraint;

- a permanent, relatively transparent standing forum for ad hoc inquiries as the need for them occurs, with the added legitimacy derived from a composition of parliamentarians rather than appointed 'great and good' external to the legislature;
- a forum for review and, where necessary, challenge of the uses to which its political masters put the intelligence resources of a nation; and finally,
- a means to make the intelligence community less (for some) disquietingly opaque and distant from the electorate and their representatives, essentially to provide a 'feel-good' factor for a population that has neither the time nor the resources to have an informed sense of the intelligence community, its abilities and limitations.

Because it was not founded on the weak ground of misinformed and misled moral panic, the ISC's political context and legal mandate have avoided the worst of the built-in paranoia that characterized earlier oversight systems in North America. That does not mean, however, that it has avoided all the traps and pitfalls with which intelligence oversight must cope, and in avoiding at least one of the inherently self-contradictory would-be functions of oversight, it has certainly fallen prey to others. What trends, therefore, can we see in the ISC's first decade, as judged against our four criteria for oversight?

'BELT AND BRACES'

There can be no doubt that, acting as a 'second filter', the ISC has managed to conduct effective review of developments in UK intelligence policy and practice. However, it is peculiar how often the Committee has reported on issues without necessarily detecting the problems and issues that they represent. For example, it has catalogued the growing range of responsibilities handled by the Security and Intelligence Co-ordinator without raising any concerns about that increased span of responsibility. This was effectively a full-time post prior to the inclusion of emergency preparedness and other responsibilities, and it would appear that the post is in danger of becoming overstretched now it has been combined with that of JIC chairman.

Likewise, there is some sense of the waxing and waning of the significance and influence of the JIC chair, but the Committee has remained unwilling to be direct and explicit about the uncertainty that may be taking hold at the pinnacle of UK intelligence administration (as discussed in the previous chapter). Its monitoring of finances and various technological initiatives have also contributed a useful independent scrutiny to the effective management of the community. However, if the Committee is really to live up to its potential in this regard, it will need to achieve and display a greater degree of independence than it has in recent years. Certainly the loss of its Investigator, without replacement, can only weaken its potential in this area, as well as the next.

STANDING INSTRUMENT OF INQUIRY

The ISC's effectiveness as a standing instrument of inquiry has been variable, arguably reaching its peak during the first Blair government, when Lord King was still in the chair. As has been noted in some detail, during King's years the ISC's *de facto* role and influence expanded slowly but steadily well beyond its original brief. However, when the Committee needed to investigate the questions about intelligence in Iraq, the performance was less solid. The ISC set itself the task of essentially inquiring whether the intelligence invoked by the government to justify its policy on Iraq had been known to be false at the time, and whether any 'undue' influence had been brought to bear on the intelligence community to reach a certain conclusion. This remit completely avoided the question of whether the intelligence had been correct *at all*. The question of whether the intelligence had been subject to 'undue' pressure was not effectively addressed.

In the first place, the ISC defined the notion of undue influence so narrowly that the actual but implicit manipulation in play – setting the intelligence community the task of making a case rather than assessing it (effectively cherry-picking their own data) – fell entirely between the conceptual cracks. In the second place, the Committee was insufficiently forceful in requiring documentation and information that might have been vital to forming the judgement on influence, most notably Jonathan Powell's notorious email to Alastair Campbell – uncovered by Lord Hutton instead. It did not clearly enough detect the fact that the September Dossier was drafted in part *in parallel with*, rather than strictly after, the 9 September 2002 JIC report on Iraqi WMD. This was found by Lord Butler instead[8] – and it is a detail that raises very significantly the possibility that the dossier-drafting process may have contaminated the analytical judgements of the JIC members drafting it. It even failed to discover the existence of Matthew Rycroft's memorandum to the prime minister's foreign policy advisor, dated 23 July 2002, according to which SIS chief Richard Dearlove had warned darkly that, in Washington, the decision to go to war had already been made and 'the intelligence and facts were being fixed around the policy'.[9]

In its favour, the Committee has been available to deploy quickly, as an increasingly experienced vehicle of investigation, for issues such as the Mitrokhin Affair and the Bali bombing. But the Committee has been most inclined to falter where interests vital to the government, such as the decision to go to war, were in question. It achieved considerably less in this latter affair than either Lord Hutton's judicial review into a tangentially associated matter (the suicide of Dr David Kelly) or Lord Butler's review. An effective statutory oversight body should certainly have been able to achieve all that Lord Hutton did, and ideally at least as much as Lord Butler, and the ISC did not.

FORUM FOR THE REVIEW OF GOVERNMENT INTELLIGENCE POLICY

ISA 1994 gives the ISC the task of examining the administration, expenditure and *policy* of the intelligence Agencies. As has already been argued, such policy as the Agencies have (outside of administrative issues like recruitment, staffing and the like) is concerned mainly with implementing the *requirements* laid upon them (with the qualified exception of the Security Service, which is rather more self-tasking). It has been argued that, *insofar* as the government of the day may be pursuing policies or actions that the legislature finds, on behalf of the electorate, objectionable, *then* a major role of legislative intelligence accountability is to review those actions and priorities and, where necessary, challenge them. This is, of course, why the US congressional oversight system devotes so much more attention to the approval of covert political action plans than to 'pure' intelligence collection. The entire ISC ethos is, however, far less concerned with hunting wild agencies than with ensuring the effective management and direction of them. In this sense, it is more useful to ask whether government policy in its governance of the Agencies and the tasks laid upon them has been appropriate or effective.

The language of the Act does not really position the ISC to challenge UK government policy regarding the use and direction of the intelligence communities (the notion of a policy *of* the Agencies being somewhat ambiguous). However, the ISC has made several very significant challenges to the effectiveness of the political direction of the communities. Most significant have been recurrent ISC complaints – under both chairs – concerning the relative activities of the topmost Cabinet and Cabinet Office committees overseeing intelligence, the CSI and the PSIS. While the JIC may be responsible for the overall direction of the UK's intelligence community, the public should rightly expect the annual national intelligence requirements cycle and the five-yearly requirements review to be approved by, and issued under, a Cabinet-level authority like the CSI.

If the UK government is going to choose one set of intelligence priorities over another, then ministers should be in a position to take responsibility for this. This is especially so if the wrong priorities have been chosen, and that may well have been the case when Britain was busily expanding and improving intelligence against transnational organized crime even while Jihadi militant networks were taking root in Britain's communities, undetected and unopposed. The UK intelligence community, like that of the Americans, had been well aware of the growing threat from Islamic militants since the early 1990s.[10] It is hard to believe that the Mafia, Triads, Yakuza and Russian mobs were ever more of a threat to the national security of the UK than the international *mujahedeen* movement, in both its Sunni and Shi'ite branches. And yet SIS's Middle East and African controllerates were pared back and re-amalgamated (they had been separate since 1964[11]), with the Security Service's unwanted and unloved counter-subversion apparatus dismantled[12] at a time when subversion was merely changing form and origin, and not simply disappearing in the wake of the defunct Soviet monolith – replacing a political religion with religious politics.

As a consequence, little or no real progress has been made in penetrating the swelling ranks of aggressive religious militants coming into the UK over the last decade, and GCHQ Urdu and Arabic abilities have been maintained at a level well below what the terrorist threat requires. If Britain's defence machinery was to be cut back under *Options for Change*, then the need for intelligence and knowing where to put one's diminished military apparatus as precisely and effectively as possible actually *increased* rather than the reverse. And yet the consequence of the UK government's post-Cold War deliberations was to hobble the intelligence community in key areas, and create the conditions for erroneous intelligence to lead to misinformed, misdirected and ultimately counter-productive military action in Iraq.

Policy judgements like the 'peace dividend' reductions, or the focus on serious organized crime and the retasking of national intelligence assets to combat it, are always going to be decisions taken under conditions of secrecy. They will not be publicly debated in the way *Options for Change* was, and so some sort of forum *outside* Cabinet and the intelligence community is essential if such measures are to receive the scrutiny that decisions of such consequence deserve. The only institutional mechanism that can perform that task, and hold ministers to account in real time (rather than a decade after the fact, as must happen today), is a parliamentary body like the ISC. But to achieve such an end, the ISC must be as independent as possible, and sufficiently resourced to undertake effective investigation and review.

'SECURITY BLANKET'

It is impossible, in the scope of a study like this, to ascertain whether or not the ISC has had a measurable impact on public confidence in the intelligence services. As we have noted at several points, Iraq has dealt a serious blow to the credibility of the UK's foreign intelligence. It seems unlikely, though, that the terrorist attacks on London in July 2005 will have the same deleterious effect on MI5 credibility. After all, domestic surveillance of terrorists is very much a passive defence, and even if one detects and disrupts a very significant eighty per cent of the attempted attacks (the figure typically cited by UK intelligence officials during the 1990s) one still has to live with the remaining twenty per cent, whether that means Horse Guards, the Arndale Centre or the London Underground. However, the fact that the intelligence community had decided that there were no cells capable of mounting an attack, and appear to have had only the most minimal intelligence picture of the network that did do the bombings, says very serious things about domestic intelligence blind spots.

The ISC is the pre-eminent external review body that can publicly address what has been going wrong, and to what degree, in British intelligence. It is not only in the public eye; because of its statutory requirement to report to the prime minister and Parliament, it is ultimately responsible to the electorate. After more than a decade it has sufficient institutional experience and influence to be able to investigate these serious issues with both legitimacy and credibility.

As we can see, therefore, the ISC has managed to avoid some of the worst pitfalls of legislative oversight. But it has also failed, in many respects, to live up to its early promise. Intelligence in the present national and international climate is more crucial than ever before, and this means that the effective political direction of intelligence, the effective management and administrative control, and public trust in the intelligence community are more important than ever before. The ISC has the potential to become a vital part of the effective protection of national security in Great Britain. But if it is to achieve that end, it is time to think very carefully about the direction and form the ISC should take during its second decade.

1. RIPA is a legislative initiative as frequently misunderstood and misrepresented as any other policy dealing with intelligence.
   At the time, commentators were quick to express outrage that the Act empowered the intelligence and security Agencies to intercept email and other Internet traffic. Such complaints completely missed the point that the Agencies had had the technical ability to conduct such intercepts *before* the Act – and without any clear guidelines or constraints. Such techniques were, at the time, employed under as close a fit to IOCA as could be managed, keeping in mind the significant differences between them and the kind of interception technology IOCA was designed to regulate. As a consequence, the Act actually *delimited* the intelligence use of data interception, rather than providing for that power in the first place.
2. Daniele Ganser, *Nato's Secret Armies: Operation Gladio and Terrorism in Western Europe* (London: Frank Cass, 2004), p. 3.
3. The Ben Barka affair, of course.
4. Quoted in Hans Born and Ian Leigh, *Making Intelligence Accountable: Legal Standards and Best Practice for Oversight* (Oslo: Publishing House of the Parliament of Norway, 2005), p. 16.
5. John Stuart Mill, 'Representative Government', in H. B. Acton, *Utilitarianism, On Liberty and Considerations on Representative Government* (London: J. M. Dent, 1972), pp. 219–27.
6. For a detailed examination of moral panics, see Stanley Cohen, *Folk Devils and Moral Panics* (London: MacGibbon and Kee, 1972).
7. See, for example, Henry Parris, *Constitutional Bureaucracy: The Development of British Central Administration Since the Eighteenth Century* (London: Allen and Unwin, 1969).
8. Lord Butler of Brockwell, *Review of Intelligence on Weapons of Mass Destruction* (London: TSO, 2004), p. 80 (*Butler Report*). Lord Butler is more concerned with the degree to which the 9 September assessment affected the dossier, but, given the make-up of the dossier-drafting team from JIC principals, the risk of cross-contamination should perhaps have been considered more carefully.

9 Matthew Rycroft to David Manning of 23 July 2002, published in *The Times*, 1 May 2005.
10 James Adams, *The New Spies* (London: Hutchinson, 1994), pp. 170–91.
11 Philip H. J. Davies, *MI6 and the Machinery of Spying* (London: Frank Cass, 2004), p. 304; *Butler Report*, p. 103.
12 Security Service, *The Security Service* (London: HMSO, 1993), p. 12; Security Service, *MI5: The Security Service*, 3rd edition (London: HMSO, 1998), p. 9.

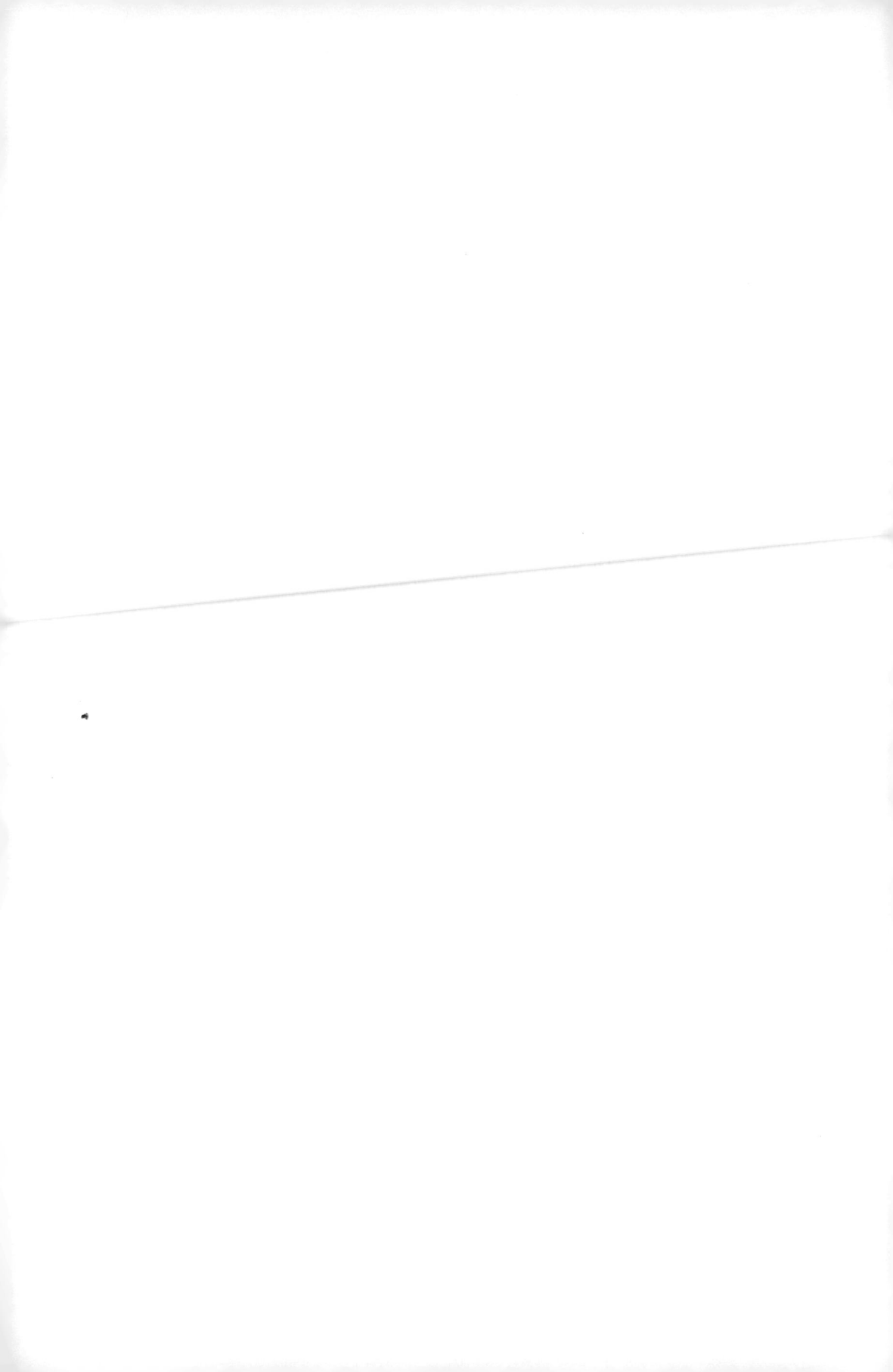

CHAPTER 6

IMPROVING THE ISC – THE NEXT DECADE

THE NEED FOR RENEWAL

We have considered the concept of intelligence oversight in both theoretical and practical terms, and have explored the possibility that it is at best worthless, and at worst a hindrance to effective intelligence activity. There are weighty theoretical arguments to support this view, but we have suggested that they do not apply in a real world of inefficiency, muddle and mistakes. We have concluded that, in the UK, intelligence oversight is not primarily a way of curbing the excesses of the Agencies (though any oversight body should always be on the lookout for illegality or impropriety), but is rather a means of ensuring that they carry out their tasks efficiently and effectively. We have identified four legitimate functions for oversight – the 'alternative rationale' which we believe the ISC fulfils.

There are many models of oversight around the world; the ISC was established as a peculiarly British way of supervising the work of the Agencies. Over the past decade and more the Committee has widened its focus, from its narrow statutory responsibilities to examine the policy, finance and administration of the Agencies, to *de facto* oversight of much of the UK intelligence community. There is a general consensus that the ISC has been 'a good thing', but after eleven years it is time to consider whether it could not be 'a better thing'. After each general election a new Committee is appointed by the prime minister, arising phoenix-like from the ashes of its predecessor. This periodic renewal should be the cue for public debate about ways of improving the effectiveness of the ISC; one of the most remarkable features of the past decade is how little serious discussion there has been of the ISC as a key part of the UK political system.

There has also been very little discussion of whether the UK intelligence community – whose core elements, as we have noted, have changed very little over the past sixty years – should undergo a more radical restructuring, perhaps extending to an amalgamation of the Agencies. Such a move would, in some ways, parallel the Mountbatten reforms of 1964, which led to the modern UK Ministry of Defence. The new ministry, however, tended towards a 'joint' rather than a wholly integrated or functional organizational structure: sections of the Naval, Army and Air Staffs with similar responsibilities remained separate within their own departments, but were brought together in joint committees. Nevertheless, the new ministry's unified approach signalled a new era in defence. By putting in place organizational structures that encouraged a new set of working practices, the relationship between the single services and the civil service would never be the same again.

Yet military operations continued to be led by one of the three services (which one was decided according to the requirements of the specific operation) until the creation of the Permanent Joint Headquarters (PJHQ), of which the MoD says:

> The Permanent Joint Headquarters (PJHQ) was established in April 1996 to enhance the operational effectiveness and efficiency of UK-led joint, potentially joint and multinational operations, and to exercise operational command of UK forces assigned to multinational operations led by others.[1]

The fact that it took 32 years from the Mountbatten reforms to establish what might appear an obvious way of conducting joint operations indicates a considerable degree of institutional inertia. Any proposal to amalgamate the Agencies or create a 'Ministry of Intelligence and Security' would, no doubt, encounter even greater resistance. While the option merits discussion (and may indeed have been foreshadowed in Gordon Brown's RUSI speech quoted earlier), we do not consider it further here, but rather assume that the ISC will oversee a UK intelligence community that will not undergo major structural change.

THE TASKS OF THE COMMITTEE

Perhaps the core task of the fourth Committee during its lifetime (which we must assume will be at least four years) will be to help restore, or even establish, trust between the intelligence and security Agencies and the British public. In order to achieve it, the ISC must begin by recognizing two substantive areas of concern – areas where, observers could maintain, it has been notably less successful.

First, the Committee must continue to address the aftermath of the failure to find WMD in Iraq.[2] As Tom King pointed out to us:

> The government is still in denial over Iraq and the public has had enough inquiries. However, in the future, the ISC should set itself the task of following up Butler.

He was in no doubt that, when historians come to write the history of the WMD issue, one important question will be 'how did Her Majesty's Government get away with it?' He argued that the ISC should carefully examine the processes by which intelligence was analysed and then presented first to the JIC and then to the government. In particular, he felt, the ISC should examine 'the relationship between the JIC and the DIS, paying special attention to how the JIC dealt with alternative views'. The line taken in public by one of this book's authors, John Morrison, was, King insisted '... significant because it was the line of someone with a professional background in intelligence'. It was also telling, King suggested, that it was Lords Hutton and Butler, rather than the ISC under Ann Taylor, who had successfully forced the government to hand over its emails for the purpose of investigation. His own experience with the ISC had been that 'if you don't ask for it, you don't get it'.

Second, in asking why the terrorist attacks on London on 7/7 succeeded, and why there was no intelligence forewarning of them or of the abortive 21/7 attempts, the ISC must grapple with the apparent failure of MI5 to monitor properly the formation of subversive organizations or groupings in the UK who were, or who believed themselves to be, part of the Al Qaeda network.[3] As we have already noted, the Security Service ceased work on subversion – as it defined 'subversion' – in the early 1990s. The ISC will need to consider whether this led to a failure to monitor domestic Islamist groups in their earlier pre-terrorist phase and to appreciate that they could develop into a real threat to national security.

It would appear that, for more than a decade, the Security Service has drawn an operational distinction between 'subversion' and 'terrorism'. But *should* there be a distinction in terms of the strategies that the Security Service ought to employ? The view of the security authorities seems to be that, in order for groups to be classed as terrorists rather than subversives, there needs to be hard evidence available of an intention to commit a terrorist atrocity (or, of course, an atrocity having actually been committed) before MI5 can intervene. The problem with this is that it is, in essence, a reactive definition, whereas any good security service should work proactively; in other words, should seek to prevent a terrorist attack from happening in the first place. Furthermore, it is perfectly sensible to argue that, before becoming a 'terrorist' (that is someone who commits violent acts for political purposes), an individual will first have become a 'subversive' (a member of an organization or group that might consider the use of terror or violence but does not currently practise it).

While the murderous Jihadists of 7/7 and 21/7 were clearly terrorists, prior to that date they were subversives. Would it not have made good security sense to have attempted to work against them in their earlier role? We would argue that the answer must be 'yes' and that the ISC should consider whether an opportunity for neutralizing them before they became terrorists was missed, in the same way that terror-sustaining 'clerics' could have been required to leave the UK before 7/7 rather than after.[4] There was, after all, copious evidence of what was going on in mosques and on campuses even before 9/11. In the same way, the Committee could consider whether 'disruptive action' should have been employed to prevent the recruitment of British Jihadists, to harry their attempts to organize, and to work against their websites.

The Security Service might argue in response that this discussion of 'subversives' and 'terrorists' is all semantics, and that they have always been alert to any real threat to the security of the state. They might also argue that penetration of tight-knit ethnic minorities is an exceedingly difficult task that requires a major allocation of resources over a lengthy period (including the recruitment of appropriate staff), and that until 9/11 the threat from Islamist terrorism within the UK did not justify such an effort. These are valid points, but the ISC needs to consider whether the ultimate result was 'too little too late'. The Committee showed in the Mitrokhin Report that it was prepared to look back many years and assign blame as it felt necessary; it is only right that the new ISC should see whether there were failures in monitoring and countering Islamist extremism in the UK.

It will, of course, be for the Committee to decide how much attention to pay to these and other substantive intelligence issues. But, looking at the ISC in the round, we believe that there are five significant aspects of its work over the coming decade that should be addressed by the prime minister, Parliament and the public:

- the ISC's status and responsibilities;
- the chairmanship and membership of the Committee;
- how the Committee conducts its business;
- how it is resourced; and
- how it communicates with Parliament and the public.

We address these in turn.

THE ISC'S STATUS AND RESPONSIBILITIES

Even before the ISC was created, it was argued that it should be a select committee reporting to Parliament, rather than a committee of parliamentarians reporting to the prime minister. These calls have continued, with even some members of the ISC uncomfortable about its unique position and suggesting it should become a select committee.[5] It is easy to dismiss claims that the Committee is the prime minister's poodle, tamely doing his bidding: many of its reports show a robust independence, not least in their persistent criticism of the prime minister for his failure to convene the CSI. But the ISC remains an anomaly within the British political system, and some parliamentarians have argued that it should either be transformed into a select committee with the same span of responsibility as it currently possesses, or that its functions should be split between the Home Affairs and Foreign Affairs select committees.

The argument for uniformity within the UK political system is weak; lacking a written constitution, the British have always improvised. But the hermetic relationship between the ISC and the prime minister does give grounds for concern; how are Parliament and the public to know that intelligence oversight is truly being exercised to best effect? On balance, and having reviewed the American and Canadian experience, we conclude that the present status of the ISC provides a 'least bad' solution to the problem of oversight:

- It is argued that a committee appointed by Parliament would be more independent than one appointed by the prime minister. This may be true in principle, but in practice the members of select committees are chosen by the party whips, with the prime minister able to influence the representation from the majority party. It is hard to see how the nominal appointment of members by Parliament would make any difference in practice, while there would still be a need to ensure that the individuals selected could be trusted to maintain secrecy. However, Ann Taylor suggested that '… it might be possible to have a parliamentary vote to endorse the actual membership of the ISC. That would constitute a simple way forward.'

- Dividing the Committee's functions between the Home Affairs and Foreign Affairs select committees would mean that the first looked at the Security Service, and the second at SIS and GCHQ. Going down this road would no doubt lead to the Defence Select Committee wanting comparable oversight rights over the DIS; it is unclear who would keep an eye on the Assessments Staff and JIC machinery. The Home Affairs Select Committee recognized this and recommended that the ISC should become a select committee with unitary oversight responsibility for the Agencies.[6]

- Paradoxically enough, a key argument against transforming the ISC into a select committee is that this would actually diminish its oversight capabilities. As already noted, in agreeing to undertake the Mitrokhin inquiry, Tom King, the then chairman, insisted that, subject to the agreement of the individuals concerned, the Committee must have access to the papers of previous administrations; with the same proviso, it must be allowed to interview ministers in previous administrations, and see policy advice to ministers. These are powers denied to select committees, but now they have been granted to the ISC, it would be hard for any future administration not to permit them again in a similar situation.

- But the key problem about making the ISC a select committee was apparent even before its creation: how could it then report to Parliament? All agree that any UK intelligence oversight body must operate within the 'ring of secrecy', but it could not lay before Parliament an unsanitized report of the type it has traditionally provided to the prime minister. It could, of course, as it does now, produce a redacted report for Parliament, but how would that improve matters? Or could Parliament select a further group (perhaps of Privy Counsellors) who would be cleared to see the full report and report back to the legislature? But that would merely push the question of trust back a step – the road to infinite regression.

We therefore see no compelling reason to change the status of the ISC. But we do believe there are strong arguments for extending its responsibilities beyond those laid down in ISA 1994. As already noted, the Committee has extended its *de facto* responsibilities over the years, but there are still four main no-go areas for the ISC:

- It has no right to receive information on intelligence sources and operational methods, intelligence operations or foreign liaisons. Note that ISA 1994 does not say that the Committee *may not* have access to such information, only that the agency heads *may refuse* to grant it. By contrast, some other countries' oversight bodies have a statutory right to complete access. The agency heads appear to have clung grimly to their prerogative of silence about these core subjects, and there is no evidence from its reports that the ISC has pressed the issue by appealing to the relevant secretary of state (who could override an agency head if he or she so wished).

- The Committee does not undertake detailed examination of the DIS and defence intelligence as a whole.[7] While it is briefed by the DIS, and visits its establishments, the ISC does not scrutinize its policy, finance or administration in the same way as it does those of the Agencies. In constitutional terms, this is quite correct: oversight of the MoD and its intelligence elements is the responsibility of the House of Commons Defence Committee (HCDC), which guards it jealously. But HCDC members are not cleared to work within the 'ring of secrecy', and hence cannot exercise the same degree of oversight of sensitive activities as the ISC.

- The ISC does not have routine access to intelligence assessments, and therefore cannot judge how well assessment bodies (above all the JIC) are performing their duties. Originally, Committee members were denied any access to JIC papers, but this absolutist position has been eroded over the years to the point that the ISC obtained full access to the JIC assessments on Iraqi WMD. But such narrow dig-down investigations cannot keep a steady eye on the JIC's performance across the board.

- The Committee has no statutory right or responsibility to examine the *government's* intelligence policies, which determine the policy of the UK intelligence community and its component elements, including the Agencies. ISA 1994 charges the ISC only with examining the policy of the three *Agencies*.

The restrictions imposed on the ISC in ISA 1994 may have reflected the Agencies' original concerns that a committee of parliamentarians could not be trusted with their most precious secrets. However, in the eleven-plus years since, there has never been a significant security-related leak from the Committee,[8] and there seems no security reason why its members should not be given most, if not all, of the complete access some of its overseas counterparts enjoy, including details of operational matters (though, as we note below, intelligence liaisons might be an exception).

Nor does there seem any practical reason why the ISC should not be given oversight responsibilities for the DIS and JIC machinery comparable to those it enjoys for the Agencies. It is tempting to go on and conclude that the ISC should exercise quality control over the JIC product, but this would be a task that would almost certainly overwhelm the Committee, and we do not recommend it. Instead, we consider that the new quality-control procedures for the JIC introduced in the wake of the Butler Report should be given time to prove themselves, but that the ISC should assume ultimate responsibility for assessing their value and effectiveness. Indeed, high on the fourth Committee's list of priorities should be a critical examination of the new measures proposed by the government in response to the Butler Committee's conclusions,[9] which, in some respects, go beyond Butler's recommendations.[10] The ISC should consider whether these measures, however sensible they may have appeared when proposed, are actually delivering the goods.

ISA 1994 could be amended to remove the restrictions on the ISC's access to information, but this would not provide oversight of the DIS or JIC machinery. We note, however, that the Act allows for the relevant secretary of state to override an agency and order that information may be disclosed. We therefore recommend that the prime minister, who has overall control of UK intelligence, should direct the Foreign Office, Home Office, Ministry of Defence and Cabinet Office – and through them the three Agencies, the DIS and the JIC machinery – to make full responses to any requests from the ISC for information, however sensitive it might be (though it should be said that there are arguments for limiting the Committee's access to information on intelligence liaisons if an agency can demonstrate convincingly that these would suffer as a result – not all our intelligence allies would trust our parliamentarians unquestioningly).

We also consider that the ISC should be given at least a *de facto* responsibility for examining the overall intelligence policies of the government of the day – its intelligence requirements and priorities, its allocation of resources to the Agencies and elsewhere, and its long-term plans (assuming it has any) for the intelligence community as a whole. We have argued that, as one of the four justifications for oversight, there is a need for a forum for the review of government intelligence policies, and it is hard to see where this function lies in the current UK system. In practice, elements of it are exercised by:

- the ISC if it chooses to do so, but this role is, strictly speaking, *ultra vires*;
- ad hoc inquiries such as those of the Butler Committee or the Security Commission, but these are only convened in exceptional circumstances (i.e. in the wake of some perceived intelligence disaster);
- the legislature, in the form of Parliament, but its debates on intelligence matters are outside the ring of secrecy, are poorly attended and have little impact;
- the media, whose approach to intelligence issues can appear capricious and ill-informed (and when well informed, may turn out to be serving another's agenda).

Of these fora, only the first two have access to classified information, and only the ISC maintains a steady watch on the UK's intelligence and security apparatus. We believe it should be prepared and empowered – either *de facto* or, if necessary, by an alteration of its legislative mandate – to examine and evaluate government intelligence policies. This would include the review of national intelligence requirements and priorities, government requirements or plans for disruptive and political actions, and other aspects of Cabinet control and direction of the UK intelligence community and its components. This would undoubtedly be inconvenient or unpopular with any government of the day, but would give the Committee additional relevance at what is, perhaps, the most crucial point in the intelligence process, and a role (and outward credibility) more comparable with existing parliamentary select committees.

THE CHAIRMANSHIP AND MEMBERSHIP OF THE COMMITTEE

There can be no doubt that Tom King, the first ISC chairman, was, in the hackneyed phrase of UK politics, 'a big beast of the jungle'. He used his experience, standing and force of character to extend the *de facto* range of the Committee in its early years, while his reappointment in 1997 as a Tory chairman of an ISC with a Labour majority appeared to send a clarion message that the Committee was apolitical.

When Tom King stood down at the 2001 election, he was replaced by Ann Taylor, a former chief whip with negligible intelligence experience. Some had expected – or hoped – that the prime minister would make Alan Beith the chairman; as a senior Liberal Democrat politician and member of the ISC from the outset, he would have continued the pattern apparently set in 1997. Ann Taylor never appeared as happy in the role of chair as did King; she told us 'I had not asked for the job of ISC chair and was initially sceptical about accepting'; she stood down from the position (and Parliament) in May 2005. Her successor, Paul Murphy, is a former secretary of state for Northern Ireland and, as such, will have had close contact with the Agencies, their product and operations. However, he is generally regarded by the media as 'a safe pair of hands' rather than a major political figure.

The downside of Tom King's dominance of the first two Committees was that other members' voices appear to have been somewhat muted. Under Ann Taylor, the ISC may have become more collegiate, but the membership can hardly be compared to that of King's first Committee. No one has suggested that the current prime minister packed the second, third and fourth Committees with yes-men, but it has to be asked whether any prime minister would willingly appoint a Committee with a membership likely to cause him substantial grief and woe.

The Committee takes its lead from the chairman, who devotes more time than any of the others to ISC business and is in daily contact with the clerk. In order that public confidence in the ISC should not be undermined by a perception (however unjustified) that the chairman could be tempted to give the current administration an easy ride, we recommend that the prime minister should, as a matter of custom, appoint a chairman from one of the main opposition parties. This would, of course, require the opposition whips to produce candidates of appropriate stature and experience.

THE ISC'S CONDUCT OF ITS BUSINESS

The Committee is free to decide how it conducts its business and which topics it chooses to examine; its one formal charge is to provide its annual report to the prime minister. Reading through these reports, there are some consistent concerns, such as the repeated failure of the Ministerial Committee on the Intelligence Services to meet. But other matters seem to last the lifetime of only one Committee and to reflect the personal concerns of individual members rather than a collegially agreed work programme.

Given that each successive Committee is likely to be made up of a mix of old and new members, the newly appointed members will face a steep learning curve if they are to become as effective as the older ones. In this context, it was unfortunate that the 2001 Committee had hardly got its feet under the table than it was required to deal with the aftermath of the 11 September terrorist attacks on New York and Washington. Subsequently, the Agencies embarked on their biggest programme of change and expansion for decades, so the ISC was tracking a moving target. This was unavoidable, but it was far from ideal. The pattern of distraction looks to have been repeated, with the fourth Committee inevitably needing to address the aftermath of the July 2005 London terrorist attacks before its six new members had had a chance to familiarize themselves with the work of the Agencies and the UK intelligence community as a whole.[11]

Outsiders cannot prescribe how the Committee conducts its business, but we recommend that it should develop a rolling strategic plan, outlining key areas of work and extending five years ahead, to be reviewed annually and adjusted as necessary to accommodate unforeseen events. This should be the result of joint discussion in the first months of a new Committee's life, and should ensure that it does not pander to individual members' hobbyhorses. The forward plan could be bequeathed to the next Committee, which could decide whether to stick with it, amend it, or scrap it and start again.

It is worth remembering that the clerk to the ISC (whose seemingly junior title conceals the fact that he or she is a member of the senior civil service) provides a strong element of business continuity and is the prime source of day-to-day advice to the chairman and the Committee as a whole. This is a position of considerable influence, and the Committee – particularly a new one – must be sure that it is pursuing its own agenda rather than that of the clerk. This is not to say that either of the two clerks to date has tried to manipulate the Committee, but, after many years in post, individuals' attitudes can harden and they can become less receptive to new ideas. The Committee must ensure that it develops its own strategy.

THE COMMITTEE'S RESOURCES

Oversight takes many forms around the world and is resourced accordingly. It ranges from the singleton post in Australia, backed by a small office, to the massive teams of staffers supporting the congressional intelligence committees in the US. Indeed, in the US it is possible to make a career as an intelligence expert on 'The Hill' or attached to bodies such as the National Security Council – that is how George Tenet, who went on to become director of central intelligence, first made his mark.

By comparison, the nine-strong ISC has minimal support – in 1999 three full-time staff.[12] From 1999 to 2004 it could also deploy its investigator to explore issues of concern to the Committee, but only on a part-time basis. In the absence of an investigator, it is hard to see how the hard-pressed staff could have time to undertake detailed research on the Committee's behalf.

The Cabinet Office's published accounts do not say how much it costs to run the ISC. Committee members are not paid for their work, though their travel and accommodation expenses must make up a considerable chunk of the secretariat's budget. A back-of-the-envelope calculation suggests that the direct personnel costs of the ISC's full and part-time support staff might be in the region of £150,000 a year – this to service a committee overseeing agency expenditure amounting to £1.355 billion in financial year 2005–06. Even a lay observer must wonder whether the ISC has an appropriate level of support. In 2003–04 the operation of the Australian inspector-general of intelligence and security (IGIS) cost the government Aus$741,000, equivalent to £318,000 at May 2005 exchange rates, of which staff costs (including the inspector-general's own salary) amounted to £285,000.[13] This suggests that the nine-strong ISC has staff support costs comparable with those of the singleton Australian IGIS.

But it is not just the quantity of support the ISC receives that is of concern; it is its expertise and capabilities. During his time as investigator, John Morrison was able to examine a wide range of agency activities, stretching from security policies and procedures through IT and R&D to personnel policies and legal matters. But he would be the first to accept that he did not have in-depth expertise in many of the areas he was charged with investigating. Rather, he brought the experience of a hands-on intelligence manager to areas where he had been responsible (albeit on a lesser scale) for the same portfolio of responsibilities as an agency head.

We suggest that more is needed in future if the ISC is to be supported as it should be. We believe that there should be a modest increase in the secretariat staff, including a relatively senior deputy clerk who could take some of the load off the clerk, and one or two in-house researchers, who could undertake document research and analysis on behalf of the Committee. Beyond this, we believe the ISC should be able to call on the service of a small panel of security-cleared experts in a number of specialist disciplines, who could be tasked (and remunerated) on an ad hoc basis. They could include experts on personnel management, organizational efficiency, information technology, scientific research and development, and legal issues; given that the National Audit Office takes an independent look at the Agencies' budgets, there is probably no need for a financial expert.

Such a panel need not be pricey, even given the fees that qualified experts might be expected to charge. But they would give the ISC an ability it did not have even when the investigator was in action – to have in-depth scrutiny of a particular area undertaken by an expert in the field.

THE ISC'S COMMUNICATION WITH PARLIAMENT AND PUBLIC

The ISC has a number of ways of communicating with Parliament and the public:

- its annual report, which the prime minister is statutorily obliged to lay before Parliament in redacted form;
- ad hoc reports that it produces on its own initiative and that are presented to Parliament in similar fashion;
- the press conference that customarily accompanies publication of the annual report;
- the subsequent annual debate in Parliament;
- any statements the chairman makes to the press during the year (successive Committees have agreed that only the chairman or an agreed stand-in should speak to the press).

This hardly amounts to transparency. It was a mantra of Ann Taylor's during her time as chair that 'the Committee does not conduct a running commentary on its activities'.[14] But no one was asking for this; rather there was a justifiable desire for an insight into the Committee's work within the 'ring of secrecy', which would allow Parliament and the public to see and judge how the ISC went about its business. In its inquiry into the Bali bombings, the

Committee took evidence from representatives of the travel industry, and in its 2004–05 annual report it describes its sessions with members of the media. In neither case could any classified material have been discussed, so why could those sessions not have been in public? We recommend that ISC sessions that do not involve classified material should be held in public, so that the world at large can see how the Committee conducts its business.

But there is a more severe criticism that can be levelled at the Committee: that it is too cautious in deciding what to publish in its reports and too ready to agree to agency requests for deletions, so depriving Parliament and the public of significant information. As an example, why can the budgets of the individual agencies not be published? Asked whether the public could know more about the figures, Tom King responded in the affirmative, though with a qualification:

> Yes they could know more, and there should be more disaggregated figures provided. However, it is important not to send signals to our enemies as to what we are investing in operations and so on. Some things are truly sensitive and must be kept secret.

If it is argued that publishing more financial details would provide information on agency activities, why is the Security Service allowed to publish a detailed functional breakdown of its activities on its web page? Just what secrets are the Agencies trying to preserve by not publishing more detailed budgetary information? What is so sensitive about the estimated cost of the new Security Service IT infrastructure project – surely this is not commercially sensitive? If the ISC can provide a breakdown of Security Service activities in percentage terms in paragraph 25 of its 2004–05 annual report, why are the corresponding GCHQ percentages deleted in paragraph 26 of the same report? If organizational details and senior staff members of US agencies can be publicly identified, why cannot their UK equivalents?

One could go on. The outside observer can only conclude that the ISC is either being over-cautious in deciding for itself what to delete or, more probably, over-willing to make redactions at the Agencies' bidding. The Committee almost boasts in the introduction to its 2004–05 report that 'To date, no material has been excluded without the Committee's consent.' Is that not in itself an indictment of the ISC's reluctance to push for more public transparency?

The Committee's caution stands in stark contrast to Lord Butler's report on Iraqi WMD, which was published in wholly unclassified form – if there ever was a classified draft, a decision was clearly made early on to provide a single, unclassified version that would include all the material Parliament and the public needed to form a judgement on the performance of the UK intelligence community (and, by implication, the prime minister). The published report provided unprecedented details of SIS operations and agents, which, one feels, the ISC would instinctively have removed from its published reports. If Butler can achieve this in a one-off report, why cannot the ISC do so routinely?

There is a robust answer, which is that the ISC, in covering all of the Agencies' activities in breadth and depth, touches on a greater range of sensitivities than the Butler Report, which covered only a limited part of the entire intelligence spectrum. It should also be remembered that much of the detailed intelligence from human sources described by Butler was subsequently found to be flawed or plain wrong, was withdrawn by SIS, and so lost its operational significance. Valid intelligence from human sources with continuing good access could not be described in similar detail without risking loss of the sources. A candid report from the ISC will therefore always require a degree of sanitization.

But we maintain that the Committee has been too ready to accept agency requests for deletions. We consider that the ISC should consciously push the boundaries, to the extent that every year some at least of the deletion requests go to the relevant secretary of state for a decision. Indeed, the fact that the Committee has so far been happy with all the agency requests for deletions suggests an over-cosy relationship between the protagonists. Better, surely, that the ISC should constantly be arguing for more transparency and that politicians should be forced to make – and justify as they may to Parliament and the public – decisions on what may or may not be revealed.

CONCLUSIONS

In researching this book, we have been struck by how little academic or political debate there has been over the past decade about the ISC and the way it carries out its duties. Individual Committee reports have had some impact (though often less than they deserve), but the ISC very soon became part of the accepted political furniture. We believe this is less than ideal, and maintain that, while the ISC has a legitimate function to scrutinize the UK intelligence community, Parliament and the public have an equal right to scrutinize the Committee's exercise of its duties. While we accept that, on a day-to-day basis, the ISC must operate in large part within the 'ring of secrecy', we suggest that this has allowed it to avoid critical examination. After more than eleven years, this risks ossification, with future Committees going through the motions but exercising less and less effective oversight.

In summary, we contend that, in order to perform its functions effectively, the ISC should retain its present status, however anomalous, but that it needs:

- authority to oversee all the key elements of the UK intelligence community, including the DIS and JIC machinery, as well as government policies on intelligence;
- a strong and experienced chairman, who should be drawn from one of the main opposition parties;
- members with proven independence of mind and ideally some prior experience of intelligence matters;
- a strengthened in-house support team, with a clerk who works to a long-term strategy established by the Committee;
- a small panel of external experts who can be called upon to undertake investigations in specialist areas; and
- greater transparency in the exercise of its duties, with some evidence sessions held in public and fewer redactions to its published reports; the Committee should consciously push the boundaries.

In making these recommendations, we are conscious that there are contradictions built in to the ISC's position that cannot be reconciled; they can only be accommodated. It is appointed by, and reports to, the prime minister; yet it must be seen as apolitical and impartial. It operates within the 'ring of secrecy' and can never report fully to Parliament or the public; yet it must convince outsiders that it is delivering an honest verdict on the Agencies' activities. It must gain and retain the faith of the Agencies that it can safeguard their secrets; yet it must not be seduced into an over-cosy relationship with them. It must renew itself every four to five years; yet it must maintain long-term oversight of the UK intelligence community stretching across successive administrations.

We do not pretend that there are simple answers to these conundrums, but we do believe they merit informed discussion. If there is one overarching criticism of the UK intelligence oversight system, it is that such a discussion has been largely absent in the past decade. We hope that this book may stimulate and contribute to the future debate.

1   http://www.northwood.mod.uk/
2   Lord Butler of Brockwell, *Review of Weapons of Mass Destruction* (London: TSO, 2004), p. 109. For a recent description of the state of the WMD issue, see Philip H. J. Davies, 'Collection and Analysis on Iraq: Britain's Machinery of Spying Breaks Down' and Anthony Glees, 'The Use of Intelligence' in *Parliamentary Affairs: A Journal of Comparative Politics*, Vol. 58, No. 1, January 2005, pp. 138–56.
3   Anthony Glees and Chris Pope, *When Students Turn to Terror: Terrorist and Extremist Activity on British Campuses* (London: Social Affairs Unit, 2005).
4   We are referring to individuals such as Abu Hamza and Omar Bakri Mohammed.
5   Dale Campbell-Savours and Alan Beith in the 1998 House of Commons debate on the security and intelligence Agencies; *Hansard*, 2 November 1998, Cols 578 and 600.
6   *Ibid.*, para. 41.
7   This does not just cover the DIS, but the collection assets for which it has responsibility, the operational and tactical elements which support forces in the field, the procurement of intelligence-related equipment, and the communications and IT systems which knit the whole together. There are no indications that the MoD has any overarching strategy for defence intelligence in the round.
8   In fact, until 2006 there had been no leak whatever. However, on 30 March 2006 the BBC had leaked to it the key findings of the ISC's investigation into the 7 July London bombings. It is not known whether the leak came from the Committee, its staff, the Agencies or the prime minister's office.
9   *Review of Intelligence on Weapons of Mass Destruction: Implementation of its Conclusions*, Cm 6492, March 2005.
10 For example, in stating (*ibid.*, para. 30) that 'In cases when the JIC cannot reach consensus, dissenting views will be reflected by the JIC Chairman in a note on the face of the final JIC assessment' some would maintain that this is an undesirable step towards the US practice of dissenting footnotes in national intelligence estimates.
11 Baroness Meta Ramsay of Cartvale might be an exception; a career diplomat in earlier life, she is often assumed to have been a member of SIS and, it has been suggested, was even considered as a potential chief of the Service.

12 *Accountability of the Security Service*, footnote 27. Though not stated explicitly, these would appear to include the clerk. It may be assumed that, as elsewhere in the civil service, part-time staff are brought in to cope with peaks in support requirement.
13 IGIS, *Annual Report 2003–2004*, Financial Statement.
14 See, for example, *Hansard*, 3 July 2003, Col. 581, where she said: 'We have said that we will not give a running commentary on our current inquiries.'